Indian Cooking

Quick, easy, delicious recipes to make at home

Indian Cooking

JAN PURSER AJOY JOSHI

PERIPLUS

First published in the United States in 2003 by Periplus Editions (HK) Ltd.,
with editorial offices at 364 Innovation Drive, North Clarendon, Vermont 05759
and 130 Joo Seng Road #06-01/03 Singapore 368357.

Library of Congress Cataloging-in-Publication Data is available.
ISBN-13: 978-0-7946-5033-9
ISBN-10: 0-7946-5033-3

DISTRIBUTED BY

North America, Latin America
& Europe
(English Language)
Tuttle Publishing
364 Innovation Drive
North Clarendon, VT 05759-9436
Tel: (802) 773-8930
Fax: (802) 773-6993
Email: info@tuttlepublishing.com
www.tuttlepublishing.com

Japan
Tuttle Publishing
Yaekari Building, 3rd Floor
5-4-12 Osaki, Shinagawa-ku
Tokyo 141-0032
Tel: (03) 5437-0171
Fax: (03) 5437-0755
Email: tuttle-sales@gol.com

Asia Pacific
Berkeley Books Pte. Ltd.
130 Joo Seng Road
#06-01/03 Singapore 368357
Tel: (65) 6280-1330
Fax: (65) 6280-6290
Email: inquiries@periplus.com.sg
www.periplus.com

Commissioned by Deborah Nixon
Text: Jan Purser and Ajoy Joshi
Photographer: Alan Benson
Stylist: Marie-Helene Clauzon
Food Preparation: Rodney Dunn
Designer: Bettina Hodgson
Editor: Judith Dunham
Production Manager: Jane Kirby
Project Co-ordinator: Bettina Hodgson
Props: Durina, Rajula Imports, Acorn Trading, Ruby Star Traders, Bison Homewares

First Edition
10 09 08 07   6 5 4 3 2 1

Set in Spartan Classified on QuarkXpress
Printed in Singapore

Contents

Introduction

As a young boy growing up in Hyderabad (India) in the early 1960s, I dreamt of eating in the Taj Mahal Hotel restaurants, famous for their masala dosai. My school was behind one of the restaurants, and passing it daily was the beginning of my love not only for masala dosai but for food in general.

After I finished my schooling, many paths were open to me, but I decided that I had to do something different. Hence I began the challenging but rewarding journey to become a cook. During my catering school days in Madras, I was fortunate to work at the Taj Coramandel and Fisherman's Cove Hotels, the former as a waiter (providing the tips that sustained me financially) and the latter as a trainee cook (giving me the tips I needed to become a chef). The next step was very clear—I had to become an executive chef.

Working at the Taj Group of hotels, especially in the banquet kitchen as a sous-chef, was always exciting. Once the food was cooked, it was displayed attractively, which brought out my artistic instincts. After hard work, and more hard work, I realized my dream in 1988, when I was appointed executive chef of the Gateway Hotel in Bangalore. This also opened up opportunities for me to explore other parts of the world and take my cooking skills offshore.

Thirteen years and six restaurants later, I am at Nilgiri's in Sydney, discovering my roots and cooking Indian food with a simple philosophy guided by the famous Hyderabadi saying that good food comes with fursat (leisure) and mohabbat (love). The food at Nilgiri's is simple, and the menu small, which allows the chefs to focus on the finer details of each dish.

Cooking Indian food, like any other great cuisine, is a celebration of life. The recipes in this book are a selection of popular and notable dishes, presented in a format that makes them easy to prepare. I hope that you enjoy the journey of cooking each dish as much as the pleasure of eating it. Finally, as any self-respecting Indian would say at the conclusion of a good meal, Anha Datha Sukhi Bhava—"May the provider of this food be happy and content."

—Ajoy Joshi

The cuisine of India, in its variety, colors, textures, aromas and rituals, reflects the flavor of the country in every way. Travelers to India feel both exhilarated by the intense chaos and confronted by the multitudes of people and the apparent poverty, while also sensing the undercurrent of spirituality that resonates on the deepest level of the culture. Whether or not you visit India, you can appreciate the array of superb dishes that represents its cuisine. And remember that you must not mistake the Anglo-Indian food served by many restaurants outside India as being authentic. Ajoy Joshi often refers to his recipes as ethnic Indian food—food that reflects the true flavor of India, and which is found prepared in many Indian homes.

Geography and history

What is formally known as the Republic of India is vast, covering an area of 1.2 million square miles (3.2 million sq km), occupied by a population that exceeds 1 billion. The topography ranges from the majestic Himalayas in the north, along India's border with China and Nepal, to the hills and plateaus in the center and south of the country, to the Great Indian Desert at the Pakistan border in the west, and includes 4,660 miles (7,500 km) of coastline along the Arabian Sea and the Bay of Bengal. With this geographic diversity comes tremendous variation in climate. The extreme north experiences snow, while in the central desert and plains, in the hot season (from May to July) temperatures of 110°F (45°C) and above are the norm. In the south, the climate is much more tropical and the temperature usually varies between 68°F (20°C) over the cooler season from December to March, to 102°F (38°C) in the hot season. All of India, but especially the south, is affected by the Monsoon from July to September, and rain is generally a daily occurrence. Visitors to India usually prefer the winter or cool season from November to March when

temperatures are more manageable for those unaccustomed to heat. The far north of India is ideal between April and August when temperatures are between 52°F (12°C) and 70°F (24°C).

India has 25 states and seven territories, and each region has developed its own cuisine in response to its history, climate, religion and local ingredients. The Vindhya Mountain range runs from east to west, dividing the country into north and south. India has been inhabited by the human race since at least 5,000 B.C. Its long history is colorful and, during some periods, violent. The first major civilization of the region, the Dravidians or Harappan Civilization, developed in the Indus River Valley (in Pakistan) over a 1,000-year span beginning in 2,500 B.C. This is where Hinduism is believed to have originated. The Dravidians left evidence of two civilized cities, Harappa and Mohenjodaro, each complete with intricate drainage systems and indoor plumbing, a ritual swimming pool, and ventilated grain storage areas. The Dravidians appeared to have domesticated animals and cultivated crops on a small scale. It is thought the decline of this apparently advanced culture occurred after the invasion of the Aryans from central Asia beginning in 1,500 B.C. The Aryans eventually forced the Dravidians south and took control of the north. It was the Aryans who wrote the sacred Hindu texts, the Vedas. The Dravidians remained in southern India and their ancient language is still used in many forms in the south today.

During the time of Aryan rule, wheat was grown throughout the year in the north of india, and rice was cultivated in the south. Therefore, wheat-based breads, called roti, became the staple foods in the north along with rice, and rice became the main staple in the south.

Around 321 BC, the Mauryan Empire took over the north and, by 262 BC, controlled a larger portion of India than any subsequent regime, except the Mughals and the British. One Mauryan emperor, Asoka, converted to Buddhism, and during his reign, vegetarianism was embraced widely, reflecting beliefs against the killing of animals for food.

After the collapse of the Mauryan Empire in 184 B.C, rulers came and went, all impacting the culture and the cuisine. Beginning around 1000 A.D, the Muslim invasions began, and Muslim armies started exerting their power. Yet even after 800 years of Muslim influence, only one-fourth of the population converted to Islam.

One of the largest Muslim influences on India was the Mughals from Persia, followers of Islam, whose dynasty dominated India for more than 200 years beginning in 1527. With the Mughal rule came a wealth of artistic accomplishments in architecture, literature and artwork. The influence of the Mughals was also felt in the cuisine, in their preference for

rich and aromatic dishes made with lamb, goat, nuts, dried fruits and a variety of spices such as cinnamon, cardamom, cloves, nutmeg, mace and saffron. Mouth-watering dishes such as biryanis, pulaos, kormas, the frozen dessert called kulfi and some sweets have their origins in Mughal cuisine. Mughal emperors built up great wealth and lived in a grand, opulent style.

During Mughal rule, Portuguese Vasco Da Gama, on his travels, came upon Kerala in the southwest in 1498, and in 1510 the Portuguese captured Goa on the west coast, controlling it until 1961. From Goa, the capital of Portuguese India, they traded Indian spices—pepper, cloves, nutmeg and cinnamon—that were in plentiful supply in this region, and took them back to Europe. The Portuguese influence on the cuisine of Goa is marked, and the dishes found here differ from those of other regions in India. Hot and spicy is the description often used for food from Goa as it was the Portuguese who first introduced the hot chili pepper to India. The Portuguese also brought to India tomatoes and bell peppers (capsicums) from the New World, papaya from The Philippines, pineapple from South America and cashews nuts from Brazil.

The French and the Dutch also left their influence as they ruled certain areas of the country, but it was the British that were to have the greatest impact of all the European nations. In 1612, the British established trading posts in Chennai (Madras), Mumbai (Bombay) and Calcutta. By the early 1800s, the country was under British rule and remained so until 1947, when, after periods of violence and strife, India gained its independence and Pakistan was partitioned. British influence is still felt—the common administrative language spoken is English, and conflict brought about by the division of India and Pakistan continues. And although Anglicised versions of Indian dishes evolved, they were not necessarily improvements on the originals.

Culinary traditions

More than 80 percent of India's population are now Hindu, with many following vegetarianism and the majority avoiding beef. About 12 percent of the population are Muslims, who eat meat. The remainder consists of adherents to various other religions such as Sikhs, Christians, Buddhists, Parsis and Jains, all of whom follow food restrictions according to their beliefs.

In such a large country with all manner of climates, each region has its own ingredients that can be grown or harvested readily. Seafood features heavily on the coast, and fish is often caught in the rivers farther inland. The west coast is especially renowned for its tantalizing seafood dishes such as the Meen Kozhambu and Shrimp Reiachado recipes in this book. Foods used more commonly in the south include coconut in every form, whether coconut oil, juice, milk or meat. Curry leaves and mustard seeds feature prominently to flavor savory dishes. Tropical fruits such as mangoes, papayas, jackfruits, pineapples and bananas are mostly eaten in their natural state, after meals or for snacks. Sometimes you might find them in sweets or flavoring the Indian ice cream, such as the Mango Kulfi recipe in this book. Tamarind and chili peppers both fresh and dried are used in abundance. Rice and rice-based dishes, such as the crisp, fermented ground-rice pancakes called dosai, are also important in southern cuisine.

In the north and center of the country, the food is not as heavily flavored. Nor is it as fiery as that in the south. Northern cuisine was heavily influenced by the Mughals, who introduced wonderful meat dishes. Ghee, Indian clarified butter, is commonly used here

(as well as in the south), and tandoori cooking, where meat, chicken and bread are cooked in a clay oven, began in Punjab. Wonderful flat breads (roti is the generic term) are famous in the north. These include the wholesome, flat chappati, puffed golden poori, flaky tender paratha and tandoori-baked naan. Rice is also often served in the north along with the all important bread.

Vegetables are an important part of every meal in every region, and the kind of vegetable included depends on the season and the other foods on the menu. For example, a green vegetable is always offered with a red meat dish. In a vegetarian meal, one would expect to be served a vegetable, one or two lentil-based dishes, perhaps a dish featuring paneer (homemade cheese) and rice and/or bread, along with accompaniments such as chutney and a yogurt-based raita.

Preparing an Indian meal

The Indian Diet

Indians generally keep in mind the Ayurvedic principles passed down through the generations. Ayurveda, which had its beginnings in 3,000 B.C, is an ancient philosophy of health and healing that is still strong today and has gained popularity in Western countries. Foods and spices are combined not only for their flavor but also for their healing properties. But, more than that, the Ayurvedic philosophy encompasses balance for both diet and lifestyle, as well as offering natural healing methods through the use of herbal medicines and massage techniques.

The foundation of every meal—rice or bread, lentils and oil and/or ghee—provides the three major essential nutrients of carbohydrates, protein and fat. The addition of spices and herbs contributes certain medicinal benefits according to Ayurvedic principles. For example, ground turmeric is widely used in Indian cooking, and it is now well documented that this spice is a powerful natural antioxidant and anti-inflammatory agent.

The attention paid to serving fresh vegetables along with pickles and yogurt-based dishes also helps to ensure a balanced diet by providing a range of vitamins and minerals. And, the pickles and yogurt are said to aid digestion. Much consideration is given to the flavors of a meal: salt, bitter/sour and hot/pungent being three of the most important. According to the Ayurvedic philosophy, these flavors must appear in every meal, though not necessarily in every dish, to create a balance of flavor. Pickles and chutneys, the intensely flavored condiments served at an Indian meal, help to balance a meal by providing any key flavors not already present. Just one or two condiments are served at a meal, and diners mix a little with the other foods. These condiments also act as appetite stimulants and digestive aids.

The Thali

Throughout India, a meal is often served on a round metal plate called a thali. Rice and portions of several dishes are laid out on the dish. In some regions, the thali meal is served on banana leaves. There are at least five different ways of setting out a thali, one for each direction in the country: north, south, east, west and center. Despite these variations, some constants should be present. Salt is an important ingredient in the thali because of the Hindu philosophy that a meal for a living soul must include salt. Traditionally, a little pile of salt is placed on the thali first, then the portions of dishes are arranged around it. "Most Hindus would pour a little water over any leftover salt at the end of the meal to dissolve it," Ajoy Joshi says, "because they believe salt should never be thrown away but should be dissolved instead. Salt, they say, is a sign of life and you can't take life. Life should only be dissolved."

When eating a thali, diners always start and finish with the staple food, rice or bread. Then they eat the other portions of food, one at a time, working their way around the thali. The different dishes are not mixed together. "If you start with the meat, then you must finish it before moving on," Ajoy Joshi says. "You can eat the pickle or chutney with the other foods, but that's all. If I mixed the other foods together while sitting across from my grandfather, he would say, 'You're a confused person. Stay focused and eat one portion at a time.' So you do one thing and finish it—a good philosophy for all of life!"

Etiquette and beliefs

Cleanliness is an essential part of the ritual of eating in India. Before sitting down to eat a meal, diners wash their hands well, whether they are in a restaurant or at home, and wash them again after completing the meal.

One major form of etiquette is eating with the fingers of the right hand, not the left. According to Ajoy Joshi, the right hand is considered to be holy, and it is the hand that does all the "right" things. Indians do not eat with cutlery and, instead, use a little bread or rice to soak up the sauce integral to many dishes. Fingertips of the right hand serve as a spoon: diners scoop up morsels and use their thumb to push the morsel into their mouths, without actually inserting their fingers in their mouths.

At the beginning of the meal, Hindus might put an offering of the rice or bread to one side and sprinkle a little water around the plate to acknowledge those who cannot find food easily, in recognition of their own fortune of having a good meal, and also to thank their god for the "daily bread."

Many Indians believe they should eat only food that is seasonally available in their region, a belief that stems from Ayurveda. For example, if they are from the south, it would not be wise to take a tropical fruit into the north and eat it there, because that fruit would not be in season. Nor would the effect it has on their body be suitable for that climate. This is a common belief shared with, for example, traditional Chinese medicine. From a Hindu's point of view, it is thought that by eating food out of season or from another region, you may invoke a god who is not normally invoked at that time, thereby causing turbulence inside your body. As Ajoy Joshi says, "Let the god lie—don't let him open his third eye!"

The beliefs and superstitions surrounding food are strong. If a man and a woman from different regions or castes marry, their differing beliefs can be the cause of conflict. This can also be a potential problem for, say, a pregnant woman experiencing food cravings; if she craves a food not in season and eats it, she may cause much conflict among the family, so strong are their beliefs surrounding food. Particular foods also carry superstitions. For example, it is a firm belief that a pregnant woman should not eat mango during the first trimester because the fruit is a potential cause of miscarriage.

Salt is surrounded by dozens of superstitions and Indians believe if salt is spilled between friends that they will experience a rift in their friendship which can only be mended by eating salt together. Some Indians even make sure that salt is their first purchase in the new year to bring them good luck.

Beverages

During their rule in India, the British, needing a supply of their favorite hot drink, tea, brought in tea plants from China to India and began establishing massive tea plantations. It wasn't long before Indians themselves enthusiastically took up the beverage, adding spices such as cardamom, cinnamon, cloves, anise, pepper, ginger and fennel to create the fragrant and sweet masala chai, meaning spiced tea. Chai is to the Indians what good espresso is to the Italians. India is now the major producer of tea in the world.

Many Indians drink water with their meal rather than an alcoholic beverage. Whiskey, rum, beer, vodka and gin are enjoyed before a meal rather than during it. The yogurt-based drinks called lassi are usually served only at breakfast and provide a nutritious start to the day. Several traditional drinks offer a welcome alternative to the overly sweet soft drinks available. They include panha (based on green mangoes and cardamom), nimbu pani (a refreshing drink made from limes or lemons and flavored with cardamom, sugar and salt) and lime with soda (a simple combination to which salt or sugar is added).

Westerners often like to match their favorite form of alcoholic beverage with Indian meals, and there are several schools of thought on the subject. Some say a well-chilled beer is the best accompaniment, while others prefer a chardonnay that is not oaky in flavor. In the end, the choice comes down to personal taste, and trial and error. An alcoholic still apple cider, a personal find, also makes a fine complement. Experiment with your favorite drinks to find the best partner for the delightful flavors and aromas of Indian food.

Planning your meal
Unlike Western cuisine, an Indian meal does not consist of several courses, each eaten before the next one is served. Instead, all the food, except for snacks and perhaps dessert, is served at one time. When planning a traditional Indian meal, you can start with one of the snacks or appetizers. Then plan to serve several dishes at once as the main part of the meal. Most of the recipes in this book will form part of a meal that serves eight to ten.

From the sections in this book, you could include rice and/or bread, a lentil-based dish or other vegetarian dish; a paneer-, chicken- or meat-based dish; a seafood dish; one or two vegetable dishes; a pickle or a chutney; and, a raita. If you're making a vegetarian meal, in place of the chicken, meat or seafood dish, include an extra lentil-based dish. However, a vegetarian meal can be as simple as one lentil dish and one vegetable dish with rice.

You can also serve the dishes in this book in Western style if you desire. In which case, follow the standard Western philosophy—a protein dish (meat, chicken, seafood or vegetarian), two to three vegetable dishes, and a carbohydrate (steamed rice, a rice-based dish, and/or bread).

Ingredients

Ajwain seeds Also known as ajwain, these tiny seeds have the flavor of thyme with peppery overtones. Similar in appearance to celery seeds, they are used in Indian breads, fried snacks, and lentil and vegetable dishes.

Asafoetida Grinding the dried resinous gum of a giant fennel plant produces this foul-smelling yellow powder. Its unappealing aroma disappears when it is added in small amounts to food, offering a mild onion or garlic flavor—a fact that caught the attention of the Hindu Brahmins and Jains whose diets do not allow the use of onions and garlic. It is also added to help prevent the gastric distress associated with eating lentils and beans along with other foods high in fiber.

Banana leaves The leaves of the banana tree are used to wrap foods before steaming or baking. Cut the leaves from center veins and pass over a gas flame or place in a preheated large, dry frying pan until they turn bright green and soften, making folding easier. Aluminum foil or parchment (baking) paper can be substituted.

Basmati rice The major long-grain rice used throughout India. This rice has a delightfully unique fragrance when cooked and complements all Indian food. Once cooked, the rice grains should not stick together but should be separate grains.

Chickpea (garbanzo bean) flour Dried chickpeas are ground to a fine yellow flour rich in protein and dietary fiber. Also known as besan and gram flour, it is used in many Indian dishes, both sweet and savory. The flour has a slightly nutty flavor and is often used as an ingredient in batters, in pastries and doughs. It is an excellent ingredient in vegetarian dishes.

Ajwain seeds

Asafoetida

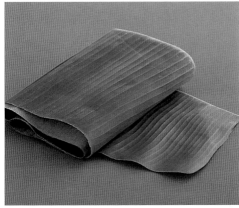

Banana leaves

Basmati rice

Chickpea (garbanzo bean) flour

Chickpeas (garbanzo beans), split

Chili peppers, fresh

Chili peppers, dried

Cilantro, fresh

Coconut milk, coconut cream

Chickpeas (garbanzo beans), split

Known as channa dal and gram lentils, the chickpeas are smaller than those used in Western cusines although the flavor is very similar. Yellow split peas may be substituted, although the flavor will differ somewhat and the split peas may take a little longer to cook. Split chickpeas are used in soups, are roasted and ground to flavor snacks and vegetable dishes, and are sometimes used in sweets.

Chili peppers, fresh We use a combination of small red and green fresh serrano or birdseye chilies in this book. Don't remove the seeds, just chop chilies very finely or grind to a paste in a small food processor. If you prefer less heat from chilies, remove seeds and white membranes before chopping or grinding. Or, reduce the amount of chilies used in the recipe.
Dried Use good quality, whole dried serrano chilies in the recipes unless specified otherwise. Don't deseed them. If you prefer less heat, decrease the number of chilies used.

Cilantro (fresh coriander), fresh

This flavored herb is used throughout India and is generally added just before serving a dish to ensure its flavor is retained. It is sold in bunches and has dark green serrated leaves on thin stems. Chop the leaves and some of the stems when a recipe calls for chopped cilantro as the stems also add flavor.

Coconut milk, coconut cream

Coconut milk is produced by pulverizing coconut meat with water and then draining and squeezing the mixture to extract the liquid. As the milk sits, the fat rises to the surface and is skimmed off to make coconut cream. This cream is canned or packaged and sold separately to the coconut milk. The cream is much thicker and richer than the milk.

Coconut, fresh Always choose a fresh coconut that is heavy for its size, and, when shaken, the juice audibly sloshes inside. The coconut flesh, once removed from the shell and husked, should be creamy white in color, crisp, firm and fiberous with a pleasant coconut flavor.

Curry leaves Native to India and Sri Lanka, curry leaves are predominantly used in the south. They are also known as karhi patta and have a strong savory flavor with a hint of citrus. The dark-green shiny, soft leaves grow on a small tree and measure roughly half a finger length. Curry leaves are used in saucy dishes, spice mixes, marinades and soups. You can use dried curry leaves as a substitute, using the same number as stated in the recipe, but make sure the dried leaves have a good color.

Garlic Used throughout India except by the Hindu Brahmins and Jains, garlic is as important as onions in many Indian savory dishes. If you are cooking several recipes that call for garlic, peel the garlic cloves then process in a food processor with enough vegetable oil (like sunflower or canola oil) to make a paste. Keep in an airtight container in the refrigerator for up to 3 days.

Ginger, fresh Another ingredient that is ubiquitous to Indian cuisine, ginger is a rhizome with a pungent aroma and warm to hot flavor. To prepare for cooking, scrub the ginger to remove any dirt, chop coarsely, then process in a food processor with enough vegetable oil (like sunflower or canola oil) to make a paste. Keep in an airtight container in the refrigerator for up to 3 days.

Indian bay leaves Despite their name, Indian bay leaves come from the cassia tree. They are larger and have a slightly sweeter flavor than the European variety. Dried bay leaves are used in certain spice mixes, and in some meat and rice dishes from the north.

Coconut, fresh

Curry leaves

Garlic

Ginger, fresh

Indian bay leaves

Jaggery

Lentils, black

Lentils, yellow split

Lentils, green/brown

Mangoes

Jaggery Made from dehydrated sugarcane juice, this sweetener has a flavor resembling brown sugar and molasses. Dark brown sugar may be substituted although the flavor will not be quite the same.

Lentils: Black lentils Also known as urad dal and black gram, these are used whole, unhulled and split, or hulled and split. They are also ground into split black lentil flour (urad flour). They are quite small compared with other lentils and cook more quickly. The split lentils become mushy when cooked. Black lentils are used in lentil and vegetable dishes, and are roasted to add a nutty flavor to savory dishes. The flour is combined with rice flour in dishes such as dosai.

Yellow split These small lentils have many names, including toor dal, toovar dal, tour dal, arhar dal and pigeon peas, and are commonly used in vegetarian dishes and soups. Smaller than split chickpeas, they have a mild, slightly sweet flavor and tend to become mushy when cooked.

Green/brown These are sometimes sold as brown or green lentils and yet are one and the same. They are generally sold as whole lentils, not split. Green/brown lentils are a little larger than other lentils, have a slightly nutty flavor and hold their shape when cooked.

Mangoes Tropical fruit used while still unripe, or when ripe. Green mangoes are made into pickles and chutneys and are used to add a tartness to savory dishes. The sweet, juicy ripe fruits are enjoyed raw or made into ice cream.

Mint These fresh leaves with a clean, refreshing taste have many uses in Indian cooking. They are used in biryani and in meat and chicken dishes, are added to raitas and homemade drinks, and fresh or dried leaves are made into a hot tea. Add fresh leaves at the end of cooking to preserve flavor.

Nigella seeds Also known as kalonji, these tiny black seeds are sometimes incorrectly called black cumin seeds and are also known as onion seeds, although they are not related to onions. The seeds have a flavor similar to cumin but with a slightly bitter, metallic edge. They are used in breads, salads and lentil dishes, and with vegetables.

Red kidney beans Known as rajma, the kidney bean holds its shape and has a slightly floury texture and sweetish flavor when cooked. Along with legumes such as lentils and split chickpeas, it provides essential protein for the vegetarian diet.

Rice flour Medium to coarse rice flour is used in dosai, the fermented rice pancakes from the south. Finer rice flour is used in idli, the little steamed cakes served with lentils, often for breakfast. The finer flour is also used in batters and some desserts.

Semolina Ground from the endosperm of durum wheat, semolina has a bland flavor and slightly coarse texture. Coarse semolina is used in the recipes in this book, and makes a crunchy coating on fried savory food; finer semolina may be substituted. Semolina, both coarse and fine, is used in Indian sweets and some breads.

Mint

Nigella seeds

Red kidney beans

Rice flour

Semolina

Sesame seeds

Tamarind concentrate

Vegetable oil

Melted unsalted butter

Yogurt

Sesame seeds The seeds of an herb that grows in India and other parts of Asia. Whole or ground white sesame seeds are used in savory dishes, breads and many sweets. Sometimes the seeds are toasted to add a nuttier flavor.

Tamarind concentrate Also called tamarind paste, this concentrate is made from the pulp and seeds taken from the pods of the tamarind tree. It is simply spooned from the jar without the need for any of the preparation that the blocks of compressed tamarind pulp require. It adds a tart, fruity flavor to savory dishes. Jars of the concentrate are readily available.

Vegetable oil and melted unsalted butter Many recipes in this book call for a mixture of polyunsaturated vegetable oil, such as sunflower oil or canola oil, and melted unsalted butter. If making several dishes, mix a quantity of melted butter and oil at a ratio of 50:50 so that the mixture is ready to quickly measure out as needed. The combination of butter and oil offers the best that both have to offer in both heating temperature point and flavor.

Yogurt The best yogurt to use for the recipes in this book is a thick plain (natural) yogurt made from whole (full cream) milk. Look for yogurt labeled "continental" or "Greek style."

Spices

Black salt Known in India as kala namak, black salt, also called rock salt, is mined from quarries in central India. Despite the name, this mineral is not sodium but is sulphur based, which explains its sulphuric aroma and its mild salty taste. The black substance turns grayish pink when ground. It is used in drinks, snacks and salads and is an important ingredient in chat masala.

Cardamom pods, Green Whole green cardamom pods are filled with fragrant, tiny black seeds. For best flavor, grind your own just before using. In this book, pods are usually ground whole. You can also buy pre-ground cardamom seeds. Cardamom is a key ingredient in garam masala and many other spice mixes, and is used in numerous savory and sweet dishes. **Brown** Not to be confused with green cardamom, brown (also called black) cardamom pods yield tiny, smoky flavored seeds. The pods are used in savory dishes and are a vital ingredient in many meat dishes.

Chat masala Sometimes called chaat masala, this tasty, tart mixture of toasted and ground spices and other flavorings is sprinkled over food just before serving. It may contain any of the following ingredients: black salt, table salt, asafoetida, cumin, coriander, dried mint, ginger, mace, garam masala, pomegranate seeds, chili peppers, black pepper and amchur powder (ground dried green mango).

Cinnamon sticks Also called cinnamon quills, these hard sticks consist of rolled and layered pieces of bark from the cinnamon tree. Those commonly available for cooking are 3–4 inches (8–10 cm) long. Many stores sell cassia sticks labeled as cinnamon sticks. Cassia, also a dried bark, has a more intense fragrance. Either can be used in these recipes.

Black salt

Cardamom pods, green & brown

Chat masala

Cinnamon sticks

Cloves

Coriander seeds

Cumin seeds

Fennel seeds

Cloves These are the dried buds of a tree that grows in Southeast Asia and the West Indies. Cloves are another key ingredient in garam masala and many other spice mixes, and are also added to rice dishes, meat dishes and sweets to contribute their sharp but sweet flavor. Buy good quality, whole cloves, which have a small stem and the buds still attached.

Coriander seeds The plant that provides fresh cilantro (fresh coriander) is the source of these seeds, which are usually dry-roasted in a frying pan before being ground and used alone, or ground as part of a spice mix. Freshly ground coriander seeds have a fragrance that is both lemony and herbaceous.

Cumin seeds These are the seeds from a plant in the parsley family. Briefly dry-roasting cumin seeds brings out their flavor, which is earthy, pungent and a little bitter. Used whole or ground, cumin seeds are a common ingredient in spice mixes, many savory dishes and raitas. Black cumin seeds have a slightly less bitter flavor.

Fennel seeds The seeds from the fennel plant, this spice, used whole or ground, contributes an aniseed-like flavor to meat dishes, vegetable dishes, desserts, pickles and chutneys. It is sometimes added to garam masala. Whole fennel seeds, plain or sugar coated, are served at the end of a meal as a digestive aid.

Fenugreek seeds Whole or ground fenugreek seeds are used along with the dried leaves; the two forms are not interchangeable. The seeds, roasted to bring out their bitter, sharp and nutty flavor, are added to spice mixes, breads, chutneys and lentil dishes. Fenugreek leaves have a subtle sweetness.

Mustard seeds Brown or black mustard seeds are called for in this book. They are always crackled in hot oil for a few seconds to release their pungent flavor. Mustard oil is a popular cooking medium in India.

Nutmeg and mace

Nutmeg The seed of a tree, nutmeg is ground and most commonly teamed with sweet foods. In India, it is also an ingredient in some spice mixes for savory dishes. Its mild, sweet flavor complements both white and red meats. The spice is thought to help tenderize meat.

Mace The red outer coating of nutmeg, mace has a more pungent flavor than nutmeg and enhances savory dishes. Blade mace is the whole coating, which has been removed from the nutmeg and dried; it has a coarse, netted appearance. Mace goes well in pulaos and seafood dishes.

Paprika Red peppers are dried and ground to produce this spice used to flavor and add color to savory dishes. Paprika is available in various heat levels; mild forms, with the flavor of bell pepper (capsicum), are used in this book.

Fenugreek seeds

Mustard seeds

Nutmeg and mace

Paprika

Peppercorns

Saffron threads

Star anise

Turmeric

Peppercorns Ajoy Joshi calls pepper "the king of spices," as it is featured extensively in Indian cooking. Both whole black peppercorns and ground white peppercorns are used in this book. Always grind peppercorns just before adding to a dish to ensure the best aroma and flavor.

Saffron threads If pepper is the king of spices, then saffron is the ruling queen. Saffron threads are the dried stigmas from a variety of crocus flower, each of which produces only three stigmas. Harvesting saffron is labor-instensive, making it the most costly spice in the world. Saffron threads are generally soaked in a warm liquid to release their intense gold-yellow color and pungent, earthy aroma and flavor.

Star anise This spice is the dried star-shaped fruit from a variety of evergreen magnolia tree. Commonly used in Chinese cooking, star anise also makes an appearance in Indian foods. Its flavor is similar to that of aniseed, but has more depth of flavor and sweetness.

Turmeric An essential ingredient for the Indian pantry, turmeric is used in most savory dishes to lend a deep gold color and sharp and sometimes slightly bitter flavor. It also tends to amalgamate the flavors of other spices. Derived from the root of a tropical plant, turmeric is generally dried and then ground, though it is also used fresh. Use turmeric grown in Alleppey, Kerala, for the best color and flavor.

Equipment

Deghchi This is a thick-based pan which is quite large but shallower than a large saucepan and traditionally has rounded sides. It's perfect for making many of the saucy dishes in this book—make sure it has a tight-fitting lid. You can also use a large, shallow, thick-based pan with a lid.

Flat-based colander/strainer The colander must be flat-based so that the paneer sits flat when weighted while draining.

Karhai pan Also known as kadai or kadhai, this is a heavy metal bowl-like pan, much like a wok, used for general cooking and deep-frying.

Katori This is a metal measuring cup for ladling dosai batter. The flat base is used to spread the batter evenly (about $1/_3$ to $1/_2$ cup capacity). You can also use good quality flat-based metal measuring cups, or a plain metal cup for this.

Muslin cloth Essential for making paneer, muslin cloth can be bought from good kitchenware stores.

Palta This is an Indian-style chan. It has a long handle and wider rounded end that fits the surface of the karhai when stirring. You can also use a wok chan if you have one.

Deghchi

Flat-based colander/strainer

Karhai pan

Katori

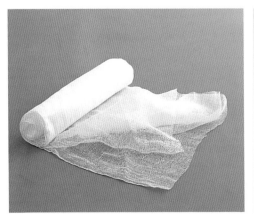
Muslin cloth

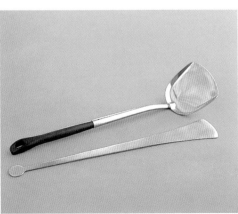
Palta

Parãt

Rolling pin

Slotted spoon

Spice grinder

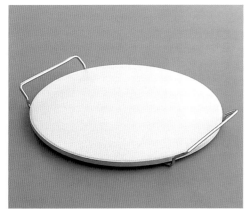

Pizza stone

Tawa

Parãt Not essential, this is a large, shallow and straight-sided metal dish used for mixing the Indian bread dough. You can use a large shallow mixing bowl instead.

Rolling pin Called a belan, this is used for rolling out the Indian breads. You can use a standard rolling pin.

Slotted spoon Essential for correct lifting and draining of deep-fried food. Don't use tongs to lift food out of the hot oil as a slotted spoon is the much safer option.

Spice grinder You will need a good quality spice grinder for these recipes. Ajoy Joshi uses a Sumeet brand grinder which has both dry and wet mix attachments. You can use any good quality spice grinder or coffee grinder (kept only for spices). For wet spice mixes, you will need to use a spice grinder to first grind dry spices and then a small food processor to finish the spice mix with the fresh or wet ingredients.

Stone Not essential, a large flat stone is used for stone-cooked dishes. Granite is the best stone to use (don't use limestone). The stone needs to be seasoned first—place in the oven and bring the temperature to 200°F (100°C) then use good oven mitts to transfer it to the sink to cool. Return it to the oven and bring slowly to 400°F (200°C). Transfer it to the sink once again, place a drop of water on the edge and if it sizzles immediately (and the stone doesn't crack), it's ready to use. Cool it and then place over a gas flame to heat. Stone-cooking is a healthy way of cooking meat because there is no need for oil to be used. You can use a pizza stone instead.

Tawa A flat iron hotplate, either square or round, used for cooking roti and dosai. See Masala Dosai for instructions on seasoning the tawa.

Ingredients

4-inch (10-cm) cinnamon stick, broken into small pieces

4 teaspoons whole green cardamom pods

3 brown or black cardamom pods

4 teaspoons whole cloves

4 teaspoons mace pieces

4 teaspoons black peppercorns

4 teaspoons fennel seeds

3 Indian bay leaves, torn into quarters

1 teaspoon freshly grated nutmeg

Step-by-step
garam masala

1. Heat a small saucepan over low heat. Separately dry-roast cinnamon, cardamom, cloves, mace, peppercorns, fennel seeds and bay leaves until fragrant and only lightly colored. Make sure heat is not too intense as spices must not overbrown or burn.

2. As each spice is roasted, place in a bowl. Allow roasted spices to cool. Add nutmeg, mix thoroughly and place in an airtight jar. Store in refrigerator for up to 1 year.

3. Just before using garam masala, grind to a powder in a spice grinder.

1

2

3

Finished recipe

Step-by-step
cooking **onions**

Ingredients

½ cup (4 fl oz/125 ml) vegetable oil and melted unsalted butter combined

3 yellow (brown) onions, halved and thinly sliced, or chopped

1 teaspoon salt

Cooking onions correctly is an important step in making many Indian dishes, and the process must not be rushed or the onions will burn. The quantities below are similar to those found in many recipes in this book. Use a ratio of half oil to half melted unsalted butter as this gives both a good heating temperature and good flavor.

1. In a large, heavy saucepan, heat oil and butter mixture over medium–low heat. Do not overheat or butter will burn and taint onions. Add onions and salt to pan. Salt helps onions to brown evenly and adds flavor.

2. Cook, uncovered, stirring occasionally, until onions are dark golden brown, 15–20 minutes. Onions will begin to color around edge of pan—stirring helps to distribute heat and ensures even browning.

1

2

Finished recipe

Baffad **masala**

Ingredients

2 cups dried Kashmiri red chili peppers broken into small pieces

²/₃ cup coriander seeds

3 x 3-inch (8-cm) cinnamon sticks, broken into small pieces

2½ teaspoons black peppercorns

4 teaspoons whole cloves

2 teaspoons cumin seeds

2½ teaspoons ground turmeric

In a large saucepan, combine chili peppers, coriander, cinnamon, peppercorns, cloves and cumin. Place over low heat and dry-roast until just fragrant.

Place spices in an airtight jar and add turmeric. Shake to combine and store in refrigerator for up to 6 months.

When ready to use baffad masala, grind to a powder in a spice grinder. Use in Lamb Cutlets Baffad (page 67).

Note: Use regular dried red chili peppers if Kashmiri ones are not available.

Sambhar **masala**

Ingredients

1⅓ cups coriander seeds

1 cup dried red chili peppers broken into small pieces

2 teaspoons fenugreek seeds

1½ teaspoons black mustard seeds

1 tablespoon cumin seeds

½-inch (12-mm) cinnamon stick

⅓ cup (1¾ oz/50 g) unsweetened dried (dessicated) shredded coconut

¼ cup firmly packed fresh curry leaves

1½ teaspoons powdered asafoetida

Heat a small saucepan over low heat. Separately dry-roast coriander, chili peppers, fenugreek, mustard, cumin and cinnamon until fragrant and only lightly colored. Place roasted spices in a bowl.

Toast coconut in pan, stirring constantly, until lightly browned. Add to spices. Dry-roast curry leaves, tossing often, until crisp. Add to spices with asafoetida. Mix well and let cool.

Place mixture in an airtight jar and store in refrigerator for up to 6 months.

Just before using sambhar masala, grind to a powder in a spice grinder.

Rasam **masala**

Ingredients

1¼ cups coriander seeds

¼ cup dried red chili peppers broken into small pieces

1½ tablespoons cumin seeds

1 teaspoon black mustard seeds

1 teaspoon black peppercorns

¼ cup firmly packed fresh curry leaves

¼ teaspoon powdered asafoetida

Heat a small saucepan over low heat. Separately dry-roast coriander, chili peppers, cumin, mustard and peppercorns until fragrant and only lightly colored. Place roasted spices in a bowl.

Dry-roast curry leaves in pan, tossing, until crisp. Add to spices with asafoetida. Mix well and let cool.

Place mixture in an airtight jar and store in refrigerator for up to 6 months.

Just before using rasam masala, grind to a powder in a spice grinder. Use in Tomato Rasam (page 41).

Reiachado **masala**

Ingredients

4 dried red chili peppers, broken into small pieces

4 teaspoons black peppercorns

1 teaspoon cumin seeds

¼ cup (2 fl oz/60 ml) white vinegar

4 teaspoons crushed garlic

1½ teaspoons tamarind concentrate

½ teaspoon ground turmeric

In a spice grinder, grind chili peppers, peppercorns and cumin seeds (without roasting) to a powder.

In a small bowl, combine vinegar, garlic and tamarind. Stir in ground spices and turmeric, and mix well. Set aside to stand for 10–20 minutes before using in recipes such as Shrimp Reiachado (page 61).

Bharuchi garam masala

In a bowl, combine all spices (without roasting).

Place in an airtight container and store in refrigerator for up to 6 months.

Just before using bharuchi garam masala, grind to a powder in a spice grinder. Use in Bharuchi Murghi (Home-Style Parsi Chicken) (page 49).

Note: This spice mix is not dry-roasted before use.

Ingredients

1/4 cup freshly ground nutmeg

3 x 3-inch cinnamon sticks, broken into small pieces

1½ tablespoons green cardamom pods

2 tablespoons whole cloves

3 teaspoons black peppercorns

2½ tablespoons mace pieces

14 star anise

Ingredients

PASTRY

2⅓ cups (12 oz/375 g) all-purpose (plain) flour

salt to taste

3 tablespoons melted butter

about ¾ cup (6 fl oz/180 ml) warm water

vegetable oil for deep-frying

FILLING

1 lb (500 g) desiree or pontiac potatoes, (about 3–4 medium) boiled whole and cooled

4 teaspoons vegetable oil

1½ teaspoons cumin seeds

1 teaspoon finely chopped fresh ginger

½ teaspoon chili powder

1 small fresh green chili pepper, finely chopped

¼ bunch fresh cilantro (fresh coriander), leaves and stems chopped

1 teaspoon chat masala

juice of 1 lemon

salt to taste

Step-by-step
samosas

To make pastry: Sift flour and salt into a bowl. Stir in melted butter. Add enough warm water, cutting into flour mixture with a round-bladed knife, to form a firm dough. Knead dough lightly in bowl until smooth. Wrap in plastic wrap and set aside for 20 minutes.

To make filling: Peel potatoes and mash coarsely in a bowl. In a saucepan over medium heat, heat oil and briefly toast cumin seeds until fragrant. Stir in ginger and then add potatoes, chili powder and chili pepper. Cook, stirring gently, for 3 minutes. Add cilantro, chat masala, lemon juice and salt, and mix well. Remove from heat and let cool.

1. Divide dough evenly into six portions. Shape each portion into an oval and roll out on a lightly floured work surface until oval is 9 inches (23 cm) long and 5½ inches (14 cm) wide. Cut each oval in half crosswise.

2. Place one half-oval on your hand with straight edge in line with your forefinger as shown. Wet a finger and run along straight edge to moisten.

3. Place fingers of your other hand in centre of the half-oval, folding sides in so edges overlap to form a cone. Press overlapped edges to seal.

4. Hold cone with open end uppermost. Spoon one-twelfth of potato mixture into cone and use a wet finger to moisten edge of opening. Pinch edges of opening together to seal and enclose filling.

Place samosa on a lightly floured baking sheet. Repeat with remaining dough and potato filling.

Fill a karhai or wok with vegetable oil to a depth of 5 inches (12.5 cm). Heat oil over medium–high heat to 375°F (190°C) on a deep-frying thermometer. Carefully place four samosas in hot oil and cook, turning often, until crisp and dark golden brown, 3–4 minutes. Use a slotted spoon to remove samosas to paper towels to drain. Serve immediately.

Makes 12 samosas

1

2

3

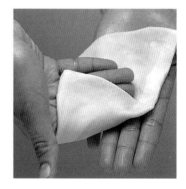

4

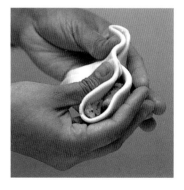

Ingredients

BATTER

2²/₃ cups (14 oz/400 g) chickpea (garbanzo bean) flour

1 teaspoon whole ajwain seeds

½ teaspoon chili powder

salt to taste

4 teaspoons vegetable oil

about 1¼ cups (10 fl oz/300 ml) water

vegetable oil for deep-frying

1 red bell pepper (capsicum), seeded and cut into ½-inch (12-mm) dice

1 medium desiree potato, peeled and cut into ½-inch (12-mm) dice

1 large red (Spanish) or yellow (brown) onion, cut into ½-inch (12-mm) dice

1 medium globe eggplant (aubergine), unpeeled, cut into ½-inch (12-mm) dice

Mixed vegetable **pakoras**

To make batter: In a bowl, combine flour, ajwain, chili powder and salt. In a small saucepan, heat oil until it begins to smoke, then quickly stir into flour mixture. Add enough water to form a thick smooth batter.

Fill a karhai or wok with vegetable oil to a depth of 3 inches (7.5 cm). Heat oil over medium–high heat to 375°F (190°C) on a deep-frying thermometer. Meanwhile, add all diced vegetables to batter and mix well.

Working in batches of about seven pakoras, carefully drop 1 heaping tablespoon mixture for each pakora into hot oil. Cook, turning as necessary, until light golden brown, 1–2 minutes per side. Use a slotted spoon to remove pakoras to paper towels to drain. Repeat with remaining batter.

Just before serving pakoras, refry them in batches of seven, turning once, until crisp and golden brown, 1–2 minutes. Drain on paper towels. Serve immediately with Mint Raita (page 107).

Makes about 28 pakoras

Note: You can do the initial frying of pakoras up to 6 hours ahead. Instead of dicing vegetables, you can cut them into thin slices, dip them in batter, then deep-fry slices until golden brown.

Split-chickpea patties

Paruppu vadai

Place chickpeas in a bowl, add hot water to cover and soak for 2 hours. Drain and reserve 1 cup (8 fl oz/250 ml) soaking water.

Place chickpeas in a food processor and process until finely crushed, adding 1–2 tablespoons soaking water if necessary to make a smooth, thick paste. Add onion, cilantro, ginger, garlic, chili peppers, fennel, cumin, curry leaves and salt, and process until well chopped and combined.

Shape 2 tablespoons chickpea mixture into a small patty and place on a baking sheet. Repeat with remaining mixture.

Fill a karhai or wok with vegetable oil to a depth of 3 inches (7.5 cm). Heat oil over medium–high heat to 375°F (190°C) on a deep-frying thermometer. Cook patties in hot oil in batches of six, turning occasionally, until light golden brown, 1–2 minutes. Use a slotted spoon to remove patties to paper towels to drain.

Just before serving patties, refry in batches in hot oil until golden brown, 1–2 minutes. Drain on paper towels. Serve immediately with raita.

Makes about 22 patties

Note: You can do the initial frying of patties up to 6 hours ahead.

Ingredients

1½ cups (10 oz/300 g) split chickpeas (garbanzo beans)

1 yellow (brown) onion, chopped

¼ bunch fresh cilantro (fresh coriander), leaves and stems chopped

2 teaspoons crushed fresh ginger

2 teaspoons crushed garlic

2 fresh green chili peppers, finely chopped

4 teaspoons fennel seeds

1½ teaspoons cumin seeds

18 fresh curry leaves, finely chopped

salt to taste

vegetable oil for deep-frying

Mint Raita (page 107) or Cucumber Raita (page 107) for serving

Ingredients

2 tablespoons vegetable oil

2 yellow (brown) onions, thinly sliced

4 cloves garlic, crushed

½ teaspoon ground turmeric

1 bunch spinach, trimmed, rinsed well and chopped

1½ cups (12 fl oz/375 ml) milk

1½ cups (12 fl oz/375 ml) chicken or vegetable stock or water

4 teaspoons butter, frozen

½ teaspoon freshly grated nutmeg

salt and freshly ground pepper to taste

heavy (double) cream for garnish

SOUPS

Spinach **soup**
Caldo verde

In a large, heavy saucepan, heat oil over medium heat. Add onions and cook, stirring occasionally, until softened, about 5 minutes. Add garlic and turmeric, and cook, stirring, for 30 seconds. Add spinach leaves to pan and cook, tossing, just until spinach wilts. Remove from heat and let cool.

Place spinach mixture in a blender and process to a smooth puree, adding a small amount of milk if necessary. Return mixture to pan.

Stir in remaining milk and stock or water, and bring to a simmer over medium heat. Simmer, uncovered, for 3 minutes. Add butter and nutmeg and season with salt and pepper. Simmer for 2 minutes.

Ladle into bowls and add a swirl of cream to each bowl.

Serves 4–6

Ingredients

4 qt (4 L) cold water

4 lamb shanks

½ bunch fresh cilantro (fresh coriander), leaves and stems chopped

2-inch (5-cm) cinnamon stick

3 green cardamom pods

3 brown or black cardamom pods

3 whole cloves

15 black peppercorns

½ teaspoon coriander seeds, crushed

4 teaspoons finely grated fresh ginger

1¼ cups (10 oz/300 g) plain (natural) whole-milk yogurt, whisked

small pinch saffron threads soaked in 1 tablespoon hot milk for 10 minutes

salt to taste

juice of ½ lemon

Lamb **broth**
Yakhni shorba

In a large, heavy saucepan, combine water, lamb shanks, cilantro, cinnamon, cardamom, cloves, peppercorns, coriander and ginger. Bring to a boil, reduce heat to medium–low and cook, partially covered, until lamb is very tender, about 1½ hours.

Remove lamb shanks from pan and set aside to cool slightly. Strain stock through a fine-mesh sieve into clean saucepan. Discard solids.

Cut meat from shanks, discarding fat and gristle. Dice meat and add to strained stock.

Reheat soup over medium–low heat and gradually stir in yogurt and saffron mixture. Season with salt and stir in lemon juice. Serve immediately.

Serves 8

Note: This rejuvenating lamb broth is traditionally served during the Ramadan/Ramzan period.

Tomato **rasam**

Place lentils in a sieve and rinse under cold running water. Drain well. Place in large, heavy saucepan with water, turmeric, asafoetida and oil. Bring to a boil then reduce heat to medium–low and cook, uncovered, until lentils are mushy, about 30 minutes.

Add tomatoes, tamarind and garlic to cooked lentils. Simmer, uncovered, until tomatoes break down, 20–25 minutes.

Stir in rasam masala, cilantro, lemon juice and curry leaves. Season with salt. Serve hot.

Serves 8–10

Ingredients

1 cup (7 oz/220 g) split yellow lentils

3½ qt (3.5 L) water

1 teaspoon ground turmeric

¼ teaspoon powdered asafoetida

1 tablespoon vegetable oil

3 tomatoes, about ¾ lb (12 oz/375 g) total, unpeeled, coarsely chopped

1½ teaspoons tamarind concentrate

2 teaspoons crushed garlic

1½ tablespoons Rasam Masala (page 32)

⅓ cup (¾ oz/20 g) chopped fresh cilantro (fresh coriander)

juice of ½ lemon

18 fresh curry leaves, torn into small pieces

salt to taste

Ingredients

2 lb (1 kg) chicken thigh fillets, cut into 1-inch (2.5-cm) pieces

½ cup (4 fl oz/125 ml) buttermilk

⅔ cup (5 fl oz/150 ml) vegetable oil and melted unsalted butter combined

1-inch (2.5-cm) cinnamon stick

3 green cardamom pods, cracked

3 whole cloves

1 teaspoon powdered asafoetida

5 yellow (brown) onions, chopped

2½ tablespoons crushed fresh ginger

2½ tablespoons crushed garlic

3–4 teaspoons chili powder

2½ tablespoons ground coriander

4 teaspoons ground turmeric

salt to taste

8 tomatoes, chopped

1 cup (1½ oz/45 g) chopped fresh cilantro (fresh coriander)

2 tablespoons crushed black peppercorns

18 fresh curry leaves

Steamed Basmati Rice (page 92) for serving

CHICKEN

Chicken **chettinad**

In a glass or ceramic bowl, combine chicken and buttermilk, and mix well. Place in refrigerator to marinate while preparing sauce.

In a large, heavy saucepan or karhai, heat oil and butter mixture over medium heat. Add cinnamon, cardamom and cloves, and cook until fragrant, about 30 seconds. Immediately stir in asafoetida, then add onions. Cook onions, uncovered, stirring often, until dark golden brown, 10–15 minutes. Add ginger and garlic, and cook, stirring, for 1 minute. Add chili powder, coriander, turmeric and salt to taste, and stir until fragrant, about 1 minute. Add tomatoes and cook, uncovered, stirring occasionally, until tomatoes soften and sauce thickens slightly, 10–15 minutes.

Stir in chicken and buttermilk and cook, stirring often, until chicken is cooked through, 5–10 minutes. Add cilantro, peppercorns and curry leaves, and mix well. Serve with steamed rice.

Serves 8–10 as part of an Indian meal

Braised **chicken**

Dum ka murgh

In a glass or ceramic bowl, combine yogurt, ginger, garlic, turmeric, sesame seeds, almonds and salt. Add chicken and mix well. Cover and marinate in refrigerator for 1½ hours.

In a spice grinder, grind cinnamon, cardamom, cloves and cumin to a powder. Set aside.

In a large, heavy saucepan, heat oil and butter mixture over medium heat. Add onions and cook, uncovered, stirring often, until dark golden brown, about 15 minutes. Stir in marinated chicken and mix well. Reduce heat to medium–low and cook, uncovered, turning chicken and stirring sauce occasionally, until chicken is cooked through, 20–25 minutes.

Stir in ground spices and lemon juice, and mix well. Simmer for 2 minutes. Serve with rice.

Serves 8–10 as part of an Indian meal

Ingredients

2 cups (1 lb/500 g) plain (natural) whole-milk yogurt

1 teaspoon crushed fresh ginger

1 teaspoon crushed garlic

½ teaspoon ground turmeric

1½ tablespoons sesame seeds, ground

8 blanched almonds, ground

salt to taste

2 lb (1 kg) chicken thigh fillets, halved or quartered (as desired)

1-inch (2.5-cm) cinnamon stick, broken into small pieces

2 green cardamom pods

4 whole cloves

½ teaspoon black cumin seeds

½ cup (4 fl oz/125 ml) vegetable oil and melted unsalted butter combined

3 yellow (brown) onions, thinly sliced

juice of 2 lemons

Steamed Basmati Rice (page 92) for serving

Ingredients

3-inch (8-cm) cinnamon stick

2 teaspoons green cardamom pods

2 teaspoons whole cloves

1 teaspoon black peppercorns

1/3 cup (3/4 oz/20 g) chopped fresh
cilantro (fresh coriander)

36 fresh curry leaves

juice of 1 lemon

4 teaspoons finely chopped fresh
green chili peppers

4 teaspoons finely grated fresh
ginger

4 teaspoons crushed garlic

2 teaspoons tamarind concentrate

1 teaspoon ground turmeric

salt to taste

2 lb (1 kg) chicken thigh fillets,
quartered

2 tablespoons vegetable oil

Chili chicken

Preheat oven to 475°F (240°C/Gas 9).

In a spice grinder, grind cinnamon, cardamom, cloves and peppercorns to a powder. Transfer spices to a food processor and add cilantro, curry leaves, lemon juice, chili pepper, ginger, garlic, tamarind, turmeric and salt. Process to form a paste.

Place chicken pieces in a glass or ceramic bowl and add spice mixture. Mix well to coat chicken and set aside to marinate for 10–15 minutes.

Brush vegetable oil over a large baking sheet and spread coated chicken on sheet in a single layer. Bake, without turning, until chicken is cooked through, about 20 minutes. Serve immediately.

Serves 8–10 as part of an Indian meal

Note: Serve the chicken with a salad made from 1 diced onion and 2 diced spring onions.

Ingredients

1 bunch fresh cilantro (fresh coriander), leaves and stems coarsely chopped

¼ cup firmly packed fresh mint leaves

5 fresh green chili peppers, coarsely chopped

4 teaspoons crushed fresh ginger

4 teaspoons crushed garlic

1 teaspoon coarsely ground black peppercorns

salt to taste

juice of 1 lemon

1½ lb (750 g) chicken thigh fillets, halved

4 teaspoons vegetable oil

Chicken **with green masala**

Galinha cafreal

Preheat oven to 475°F (240°C/Gas 9).

Place cilantro, mint, chili pepper, ginger, garlic, peppercorns and salt in a food processor. Process to form a thick paste, adding enough lemon juice to moisten ingredients.

In a glass or ceramic bowl, combine paste with chicken. Mix well to coat chicken and set aside to marinate for 20 minutes.

Brush vegetable oil over a large baking sheet. Place chicken on sheet in a single layer. Bake, without turning, until chicken is cooked through, 20–25 minutes.

Serves 8–10 as part of an Indian meal

Home-style parsi chicken

Bharuchi murghi

In a spice grinder, grind chickpeas and chili pepper to a powder. Place coconut and peanuts in a food processor and process until finely minced. Add chickpea mixture and process until combined. Set aside.

In a deghchi or large frying pan, heat oil over medium–low heat. Add onions and 1 teaspoon salt and cook, stirring often, until onions are dark golden brown, 10–15 minutes. Add coconut mixture and cook, stirring often, for 5 minutes.

Stir in coconut milk and water, and mix well. Add chicken pieces and bring to a simmer. Cover and cook, stirring occasionally, until chicken is cooked through, 20–30 minutes.

Using tongs, remove chicken pieces to a plate. Add yogurt, lemon juice and bharuchi garam masala to pan, and mix well until heated through. Taste and add salt if necessary. Return chicken to pan and turn to coat in sauce. Serve immediately.

Serves 10 as part of an Indian meal

Ingredients

4 teaspoons split chickpeas (garbanzo beans)

7 dried red chili peppers, broken into smaller pieces

peeled flesh from 1 fresh coconut (about 12 oz/375 g), coarsely chopped

¼ cup (1 oz/30 g) unsalted roasted peanuts

⅓ cup (2⅔ fl oz/80 ml) vegetable oil

2 yellow (brown) onions, halved and thinly sliced

1 teaspoon salt, plus extra salt to taste

1⅔ cups (13 fl oz/400 ml) coconut milk

¾ cup (6 fl oz/180 ml) water

3 lb (1.5 kg) whole chicken, cut into 12 pieces

¾ cup (6 oz/180 g) plain (natural) whole-milk yogurt, whisked

juice of 1 lemon

4 teaspoons Bharuchi Garam Masala (page 33)

Butter chicken

Cut chicken fillets into quarters. In a glass or ceramic bowl, combine chicken with 4 teaspoons vinegar or lemon juice, and turn to coat. Set aside.

In a spice grinder, grind coriander seeds, cinnamon, cardamom and cloves to a powder. Place in a bowl and combine with turmeric, chili powder, paprika, nutmeg, mace, remaining vinegar or lemon juice, yogurt, garlic, ginger and oil, and mix well. Season with salt and add to chicken. Mix well, cover and place in refrigerator to marinate for 30 minutes.

Preheat oven to 475°F (240°C/Gas 9). Oil a shallow roasting pan and place chicken pieces in pan in a single layer. Bake, without turning, for 12 minutes. Remove from oven and set aside.

To make sauce: In a deghchi or large frying pan, heat oil and butter mixture over medium–low heat. Add onions and 1 teaspoon salt, and cook, uncovered, stirring occasionally, until onions are dark golden brown, 15–20 minutes. Add ginger and garlic, and cook, stirring, for 2 minutes. Add chili powder, turmeric and chili pepper, and cook for 1 minute. Add tomatoes and cook, uncovered, stirring often, until tomatoes are soft, 5–10 minutes.

Add cream and butter to pan, and cook, stirring, until butter melts. Stir in chicken, honey and fenugreek, and cook, stirring often, until chicken is cooked through, about 5 minutes. Stir in cilantro. Taste and add salt if necessary. Serve immediately.

Serves 10 as part of an Indian meal

Ingredients

2 lb (1 kg) chicken thigh fillets

1/4 cup (2 fl oz/60 ml) white vinegar or lemon juice

1/3 cup coriander seeds

2-inch (5-cm) cinnamon stick, broken into smaller pieces

5 brown or black cardamom pods

10 green cardamom pods

1 teaspoon whole cloves

3 teaspoons ground turmeric

2 teaspoons chili powder

2 teaspoons paprika

1 teaspoon ground nutmeg

1 teaspoon ground mace

1/4 cup (2 oz/60 g) plain (natural) whole-milk yogurt

2 1/2 tablespoons crushed garlic

2 1/2 tablespoons grated fresh ginger

2 1/2 tablespoons vegetable oil

salt to taste

SAUCE

1/2 cup (4 fl oz/125 ml) vegetable oil and melted unsalted butter combined

2 lb (1 kg) yellow (brown) onions, (about 6 medium), chopped

1 teaspoon salt, plus extra salt to taste

2 1/2 tablespoons grated fresh ginger

2 1/2 tablespoons crushed garlic

2 teaspoons chili powder

3 teaspoons ground turmeric

2 teaspoons chopped fresh green chili peppers

2 lb (1 kg) tomatoes, (about 7 medium), chopped and pureed in blender or food processor

2/3 cup (5 fl oz/150 ml) heavy (double) cream

1/4 cup (2 oz/60 g) unsalted butter

4 teaspoons honey

2 tablespoons dried fenugreek leaves

1/3 cup (1/2 oz/15 g) chopped fresh cilantro (fresh coriander)

Ingredients

3 lb (1.5 kg) soft-shell or blue swimmer crabs

⅓ cup coriander seeds

1 cup (8 fl oz/250 ml) vegetable oil and melted unsalted butter combined

1-inch (2.5-cm) cinnamon stick

3 green cardamom pods

3 whole cloves

2 lb (1 kg) yellow (brown) onions, (about 6 medium), chopped

1 teaspoon salt, plus extra salt to taste

2½ tablespoons grated fresh ginger

2½ tablespoons crushed garlic

4 teaspoons chili powder

4 teaspoons ground turmeric

2 lb (1 kg) tomatoes, (about 7 medium), unpeeled, finely chopped

1 cup (1½ oz/45 g) chopped fresh cilantro (fresh coriander)

18 fresh curry leaves, torn into pieces

4 teaspoons crushed black peppercorns

Steamed Basmati Rice (page 92) for serving

SEAFOOD

Step-by-step
Crab chettinad

1. Remove large top shell from each crab. Remove fibrous matter from inside crab and discard.

2. Rinse crabs well. Use a sharp knife to cut each crab in quarters. Set aside.

In a spice grinder, grind coriander seeds to a powder. Set aside.

In a deghchi or large frying pan, heat oil and butter mixture over low heat. Add cinnamon, cardamom and cloves. Cook until fragrant, about 30 seconds. Add onions and 1 teaspoon salt, and cook, uncovered, stirring often, until onions are dark golden brown, 15–20 minutes.

Add ginger and garlic, and cook for 1 minute. Add ground coriander, chili powder and turmeric, and cook, stirring, for 1 minute. Add tomatoes and cook, uncovered, stirring often, until tomatoes are cooked and soft, about 10 minutes. Add crab and cook, covered, turning pieces occasionally, until crab shells turn red and meat is just cooked, 15–20 minutes.

Use tongs to remove crab pieces to a plate. Add cilantro, curry leaves and peppercorns to sauce in pan, mixing well. Taste and add salt if desired. Return crab pieces to pan and turn to coat with sauce, then serve.

Serves 8 as part of an Indian meal

1

2

Fish in coconut sauce
Meen kozhambu

Remove skin from fish fillets then cut into ¾-inch x 2-inch (2-cm x 5-cm) pieces. Set aside.

In a karhai or wok, heat oil over low heat. Add mustard seeds and cook until seeds crackle, about 30 seconds. Add fenugreek seeds and chili peppers, and cook, stirring, until seeds turn light golden brown and chili peppers are deep golden brown, about 30 seconds. Add onions and cook, stirring, until slightly softened, about 1 minute. Add ginger and garlic, and cook, stirring, for 1 minute. Add curry leaves, turmeric and chili powder, and cook, stirring, for 30 seconds. Add tomatoes and cook until tomatoes are slightly soft, about 3 minutes. Stir in coconut cream and tamarind, and season with salt.

Stir in fish pieces and simmer, covered, until fish is just cooked through, about 5 minutes. Stir in lemon juice. Serve immediately with rice.

Serves 8 as part of an Indian meal

Ingredients

- 1 lb (500 g) white-fleshed fish fillets, such as snapper, barramundi or ocean perch
- 3 tablespoons vegetable oil
- 1 teaspoon brown or black mustard seeds
- ½ teaspoon fenugreek seeds
- 3 dried red chili peppers
- 1 lb (500 g) yellow (brown) onions, (about 3 medium), halved and thinly sliced
- 2 tablespoons grated fresh ginger
- 2 tablespoons crushed garlic
- 36 fresh curry leaves
- 3 teaspoons ground turmeric
- 2–4 tablespoons chili powder
- 2 tomatoes, unpeeled, coarsely chopped
- 1½ cups (12 fl oz/375 ml) coconut cream
- 1 teaspoon tamarind concentrate
- salt to taste
- juice of ½ lemon
- Steamed Basmati Rice (page 92) for serving

Goan **fish**

Ingredients

1–1½ cups dried red chili peppers broken into small pieces

⅓ cup coriander seeds

¼ cup cumin seeds

¾ cup (6 fl oz/180 ml) white vinegar

1 tablespoon finely grated fresh ginger

1 tablespoon crushed garlic

2 teaspoons ground turmeric

½ cup (4 fl oz/125 ml) vegetable oil and melted unsalted butter combined

1 lb (500 g) yellow (brown) onions, (about 3 medium), halved and sliced

2 large tomatoes, unpeeled, quartered

2 fresh green chili peppers, slit lengthwise

2½ cups (20 fl oz/625 ml) coconut milk

salt to taste

2 lb (1 kg) white-fleshed fish fillets such as snapper, ling, cod or ocean perch

Steamed Basmati Rice (page 92) for serving

In a spice grinder, grind dried chili pepper, coriander seeds and cumin seeds to a powder. Place in a bowl and combine with vinegar, ginger, garlic and turmeric to form a paste. Set aside.

In a large karhai or wok, heat oil and butter mixture over medium–low heat. Add onions and cook, uncovered, stirring often, until soft, about 10 minutes. Add spice paste and cook, stirring, until fragrant, about 3 minutes. Add tomatoes, green chili peppers and coconut milk, and cook, uncovered, stirring often, until tomatoes soften, about 5 minutes. Season with salt.

If fish fillets are large, cut into serving-sized pieces. Add fish to sauce and cook, uncovered, until fish flakes when tested with a fork, about 5 minutes. Serve hot with steamed rice.

Serves 8–10 as part of an Indian meal

Note: Adjust dried chili pepper according to your taste—the full quantity makes a hot dish.

Step-by-step
Fish steamed in banana leaves
Patra ni machchi

Ingredients

peeled flesh from 1 fresh coconut (about 12 oz/375 g), coarsely chopped

6 fresh green chili peppers, coarsely chopped

2/3 cup (1 oz/30 g) chopped fresh cilantro (fresh coriander)

1/2 cup (3/4 oz/20 g) chopped fresh mint

1/4 cup (2 fl oz/60 ml) vegetable oil

2 teaspoons crushed garlic

1/2 teaspoon ground turmeric

1 teaspoon cumin seeds

juice of 2 limes

1/4 teaspoon sugar

salt to taste

5 fresh banana leaves, center veins removed

2 lb (1 kg) large, white-fleshed fish fillets such as barramundi, ocean perch or snapper, cut into 10 serving-sized portions

lime wedges for serving

Place coconut, chili pepper, cilantro, mint, oil, garlic, turmeric, cumin seeds, lime juice, sugar and salt in a food processor and process until finely minced to make a coconut chutney. Divide evenly into 10 portions and set aside.

Slowly pass each banana leaf over a medium–high gas flame until leaf turns bright green. Alternatively, heat a heavy frying pan over medium–high heat, place leaf in pan and heat until leaf turns bright green. Let leaves cool and cut into pieces large enough to wrap a fish portion each.

1. Place a fish piece on a banana leaf piece. Spread a portion of coconut chutney over the fish.

2. Wrap leaf around fish and tie with kitchen twine to secure. Repeat with remaining fish pieces, banana leaves and coconut chutney.

Place fish parcels in a large bamboo steamer over a large wok half filled with boiling water. Steam until fish flakes when tested with a fork, 12–15 minutes. Serve hot with lime wedges.

Serves 10 as part of an Indian meal

Note: Heating banana leaves makes them malleable and easy to fold. If banana leaves are unavailable, use parchment (baking) paper or aluminum foil.

1

2

Ingredients

¼ cup coriander seeds

1–2 tablespoons vegetable oil

4 teaspoons finely grated fresh
  ginger

4 teaspoons crushed garlic

4 teaspoons tamarind concentrate

2–4 teaspoons chili powder

2 teaspoons fennel seeds

1 teaspoon ground turmeric

18 fresh curry leaves, finely chopped

salt to taste

2 lb (1 kg) medium shrimp
  (prawns), peeled and deveined

vegetable oil for deep-frying

1 cup (6 oz/180 g) coarse semolina

juice of 1 lemon

Semolina-crusted shrimp

Karwari shrimp

In a spice grinder, grind coriander seeds to a powder. Place in a bowl and combine with 1–2 tablespoons oil, ginger, garlic, tamarind, chili powder, fennel seeds, turmeric, curry leaves and salt to form a paste.

Add shrimp to spice paste and mix well until coated. Set aside to marinate for 5 minutes.

Fill a karhai or wok with vegetable oil to a depth of 2 inches (5 cm) and heat over medium heat to 375°F (190°C) on a deep-frying thermometer. While oil is heating, dip shrimp, one at a time, in semolina to coat. Fry shrimp in batches until light golden, 1–2 minutes. Use a slotted spoon to remove shrimp to paper towels to drain.

Drizzle shrimp with lemon juice and serve hot.

Serves 8–10 as part of an Indian meal

Portuguese-style shrimp

Shrimp reiachado

Ingredients

1 recipe Reiachado Masala
   (page 32)

2 lb (1 kg) medium shrimp
   (prawns), peeled and deveined

2 tablespoons vegetable oil

juice of 1 lemon

In a glass or ceramic bowl, combine reiachado masala and shrimp and mix well to coat shrimp. Set aside to marinate for 5 minutes.

In frying pan, heat oil over medium–low heat until hot. Cook shrimp in batches, turning once, until browned, about 1–2 minutes. Take care not to scorch marinade.

Drizzle cooked shrimp with lemon juice and serve hot.

Serves 8–10 as part of an Indian meal

Variation

Lightly brush shrimp with reichado masala. Cook shrimp in batches as above and set aside. In small saucepan, heat 2 tablespoons vegetable oil over medium–high heat. Cook 20 curry leaves—or as many as desired—until fragrant, about 30 seconds. Drain on paper towels and toss with shrimp. If desired, add thinly sliced red (Spanish) onion for color.

Ingredients

5 dried red chili peppers, broken into small pieces

1 teaspoon cumin seeds

1 tablespoon black peppercorns

1½ tablespoons finely grated fresh ginger

1½ tablespoons crushed garlic

½ teaspoon ground turmeric

¾ cup (6 fl oz/180 ml) vegetable oil and melted unsalted butter combined

1½ lb (750 g) yellow (brown) onions, (about 4½ medium), finely chopped

1 teaspoon salt, plus extra salt to taste

2 lb (1 kg) beef chuck, excess fat removed, cut into 1½-inch (4-cm) pieces

about 4 cups (32 fl oz/1 L) water

4 fresh green chili peppers, slit lengthwise

½ cup (4 fl oz/125 ml) white vinegar

½ teaspoon tamarind concentrate

½ teaspoon sugar

Steamed Basmati Rice (page 92) for serving

MEAT

Beef vindaloo
Bife vindalho

In a spice grinder, grind dried chili pepper, cumin seeds and peppercorns to a powder. Place in a bowl and combine with ginger, garlic and turmeric. Set aside.

In a karhai or frying pan, heat oil and butter mixture over medium–low heat. Add onions and 1 teaspoon salt, and cook, uncovered, stirring often, until onions are dark golden brown, 20–25 minutes. Raise heat to medium–high and add beef. Cook, turning beef pieces, for 5 minutes. Add spice mixture and cook, stirring, until fragrant, about 2 minutes.

Pour in enough water to cover beef. Add chili peppers and bring to a simmer. Cook over low heat, partially covered, stirring occasionally, until liquid is reduced by half, about 1 hour.

Stir in vinegar, tamarind and sugar. Taste and add salt if necessary. Cook, uncovered, until sauce reduces and thickens, about 30 minutes. Serve hot with steamed rice.

Serves 8–10 as part of an Indian meal

Lamb **biryani**

Kachche gosht ki biryani

Preheat oven to 475°F (240°C/Gas 9).

In a glass or ceramic bowl, combine onions with 1 teaspoon salt. Set aside for 10 minutes.

In large deghchi or large, deep ovenproof saucepan, heat oil and butter mixture over medium–low heat. Add onions and cook, uncovered, stirring often, until onions are dark golden brown, 20–25 minutes. Strain onions and reserve oil and butter mixture. Let onions cool slightly.

While onions are cooking, prepare crust. Place flour in a bowl and add enough water to form a soft dough. Knead gently in bowl until smooth. Cover and set aside.

In a large glass or ceramic bowl, combine yogurt, cilantro, mint, chili pepper, ginger, garlic, garam masala, chili powder and turmeric. Season with salt. Add cooked onions, lamb, and saffron mixture, and mix well. Spread lamb mixture in base of deghchi or saucepan.

Drain rice and place in a large saucepan with enough boiling water to cover. Season with salt. Bring to a boil over high heat and cook, uncovered, for 7 minutes. Drain excess water from rice. Spread rice evenly over lamb mixture. Pour reserved oil and butter mixture evenly over rice. Cover tightly with lid. Roll crust dough into a thin sausage shape, long enough to extend around top edge of deghchi or saucepan. Place dough around edge, molding it to seal lid.

Place deghchi or saucepan over medium–high heat for 5 minutes, then transfer to oven. Reduce oven temperature to 400°F (200°C/Gas 6) and cook for 40 minutes. Remove from oven and let stand 15 minutes before breaking away crust and removing lid. Either serve from pan or place a large platter over deghchi or saucepan and then very carefully invert biryani onto platter (you will need two people to do this). Serve immediately drizzled with lemon juice and accompanied by churri.

Serves 10–12 as part of an Indian meal

Note: A long piece of aluminum foil can be used, "scrunched" around top edge of deghchi or saucepan, to create a seal in place of crust.

Ingredients

- 4 yellow (brown) onions, halved and thinly sliced
- 1 teaspoon salt, plus extra salt to taste
- 1 cup (8 fl oz/250 ml) vegetable oil and melted unsalted butter combined
- 1¼ cups (10 oz/300 g) plain (natural) whole-milk yogurt
- 1 cup (1½ oz/45 g) chopped fresh cilantro (fresh coriander)
- 1 cup (1½ oz/45 g) chopped fresh mint
- 6 fresh green chili peppers, chopped
- 1½ tablespoons finely grated fresh ginger
- 1½ tablespoons crushed garlic
- 1½ tablespoons Garam Masala (page 28)
- 2 tablespoons chili powder
- 1½ tablespoons ground turmeric
- 2 lb (1 kg) boneless lamb shoulder, diced
- pinch saffron threads soaked in 2 tablespoons hot milk for 10 minutes
- 2 lb (1 kg) basmati rice, rinsed and soaked in cold water to cover for 20 minutes
- boiling water
- juice of 1 lemon
- Churri (page 106) for serving

CRUST

- 3 cups (15 oz /450 g) whole wheat (wholemeal) flour
- about 1 cup (8 fl oz/250 ml) water

Ingredients

1-inch (2.5-cm) cinnamon stick

1 teaspoon black peppercorns

1 teaspoon finely grated fresh ginger

1 teaspoon crushed garlic

6 fresh green chili peppers, crushed to a paste

½ teaspoon salt

2 lb (1 kg) lamb cutlets

vegetable oil for brushing

2 red (spanish) or yellow (brown) onions, thinly sliced into rings, for serving

1 cup (1 oz/30 g) fresh mint leaves, for serving

8–10 lemon wedges, for serving

Stone-cooked lamb cutlets
Pathar ka gosht

Prepare a fire in a grill (barbecue), preferably charcoal.

In a spice grinder, grind cinnamon and peppercorns to a powder. Place in a bowl and combine with ginger, garlic, chili pepper and salt.

Rub mixture over both sides of lamb cutlets and set aside to marinate for 30 minutes.

On a grill (barbecue) rack, place a granite slab that is 2½ inches (7 cm) thick and about 12 inches (30 cm) long and 10 inches (25 cm) wide. When slab is hot, brush oil over surface and place cutlets on top. Cook lamb, brushing with oil when necessary, until cooked to your liking, 3–4 minutes per side.

Serve hot, topped with onion rings and mint leaves and accompanied by lemon wedges.

Serves 8–10 as part of an Indian meal

Note: If a granite stone is unavailable, cook lamb on a heavy grill (barbecue) plate or on a heated pizza stone.

Lamb cutlets **baffad**

In a heavy saucepan, heat oil and butter mixture over medium–low heat. Add onions and salt, and cook, uncovered, stirring often, until onions are dark golden brown, 10–15 minutes. Add ginger, garlic and baffad masala, and cook, stirring, until fragrant, about 1 minute.

Add tomatoes and vinegar to pan, and mix well, adding 1–2 tablespoons water to moisten mixture if necessary. Add lamb cutlets and turn to coat with sauce. Reduce heat to low and cook uncovered, stirring often and turning lamb, adding a tablespoon or two of water if sauce begins to dry, until lamb is cooked to your liking and sauce is thick, 15–20 minutes.

Squeeze lemon juice over lamb and serve hot with chappati.

Serves 6–8 as part of an Indian meal

Ingredients

¼ cup (2 fl oz/60 ml) vegetable oil and melted unsalted butter combined

2 yellow (brown) onions, chopped

½ teaspoon salt

2 tablespoons finely grated fresh ginger

2 tablespoons crushed garlic

3 tablespoons Baffad Masala (page 30)

2 tomatoes, unpeeled, chopped

4 teaspoons white vinegar

2 lb (1 kg) lamb cutlets

juice of ½ lemon

6–8 Chappati (page 98)

Ingredients

2 lb (1 kg) lamb shoulder, diced

2 cups (1 lb/500 g) plain (natural) whole-milk yogurt, whisked

1 teaspoon salt, plus extra salt to taste

²/₃ cup (5 fl oz/150 ml) vegetable oil and melted unsalted butter combined

1-inch (2.5-cm) cinnamon stick

20 green cardamom pods

5 brown or black cardamom pods

1 teaspoon whole cloves

2 lb (1 kg) yellow (brown) onions, (about 6 medium), chopped

2 tablespoons finely grated fresh ginger

2 tablespoons crushed garlic

4 teaspoons chili powder

2 teaspoons ground turmeric

¹/₃ cup (½ oz/15 g) chopped fresh cilantro (fresh coriander)

1½ teaspoons Garam Masala (page 28)

Steamed Basmati Rice (page 92) or Paratha (page 101) for serving

Lamb **roganjosh**

In a large bowl, combine lamb, yogurt and ½ teaspoon salt, and mix well. Set aside for 10 minutes.

In a large karhai or frying pan, heat oil and butter mixture over medium heat. Add cinnamon, cardamom and cloves, and cook, stirring, until fragrant, about 30 seconds. Add onions and ½ teaspoon salt, and cook over medium–low heat, uncovered, stirring often, until onions are golden brown, 20–25 minutes.

Add ginger and garlic and cook, stirring, for 30 seconds. Drain away any excess oil and butter, leaving onions and spices in pan.

Add lamb and yogurt mixture, chili powder and turmeric to pan, and mix well. Cook over low heat, covered, until lamb is tender, 45–60 minutes. Add cilantro and garam masala, and mix well. Taste and add salt if necessary. Serve hot with steamed rice or paratha.

Serves 8–10 as part of an Indian meal

Note: You can use goat meat in place of lamb.

Ingredients

4 qt (4 L) whole (full cream) milk

1²/₃ cups (13 fl oz/400 ml) heavy (double) cream

²/₃ cup (5 fl oz/150 ml) white vinegar

1

2

3

Step-by-step
cottage cheese
Paneer

Line a large, flat-bottomed sieve with a double layer of cheesecloth (muslin), allowing it to overhang sides of sieve. Place lined sieve inside a large other bowl. Choose a large, heavy, non-aluminum saucepan that fits inside the sieve.

Pour milk into the saucepan and bring slowly to a boil over medium heat. When milk is almost boiling, stir in cream and bring to a boil again. When milk mixture just comes to a boil (it will begin to bubble and froth, and vibrations from boiling mixture can be felt in the handle of a metal spoon held in milk), pour in vinegar and remove from heat. Set aside for 2 minutes; do not stir.

1. Using a large slotted spoon or spoon-shaped strainer, gently lift curds from whey and place in lined sieve.

2. Once all curds have been placed in sieve, carefully tie loose ends of cheesecloth together to form curds into a thick, round disk about 10 inches (25 cm) in diameter.

3. Return whey in bowl back to saucepan holding remainder of whey. Place saucepan on top of paneer to weight it. Set aside at room temperature until paneer is firm, about 25 minutes.

Remove saucepan from paneer. Carefully untie cheesecloth and remove paneer. Prepare as directed in individual recipes. If not using paneer immediately, place flat in an airtight container and add enough whey to cover. Store in refrigerator for up to 1 week.

Marinated baked **cottage cheese**

Paneer tikka

Preheat oven to 475°F (240°C/Gas 9).

In a large bowl, combine yogurt, ginger, garlic, chili pepper, saffron and milk mixture, 4 teaspoons oil and salt. Add paneer pieces and gently turn to coat with marinade. Set aside paneer to marinate for 10 minutes.

Brush a baking sheet with vegetable oil. Place paneer pieces on sheet in a single layer. Bake, without turning, until golden on edges, about 15 minutes.

Place paneer in a serving dish, sprinkle with chat masala and cilantro, and drizzle with lemon juice. Serve hot with a salad of fresh greens.

Serves 8–10 as part of an Indian meal

Ingredients

1 cup (8 oz/250 g) plain (natural) whole-milk yogurt, whisked

1½ tablespoons finely grated fresh ginger

1½ tablespoons crushed garlic

2 fresh green chili peppers, finely chopped

large pinch saffron threads soaked in 1½ tablespoons hot milk for 10 minutes

4 teaspoons vegetable oil, plus extra oil for brushing

½ teaspoon salt

1 recipe Paneer (page 70), cut into 1-inch x 3-inch (2.5-cm x 7.5-cm) pieces

pinch chat masala

⅓ cup (1 oz/30 g) chopped fresh cilantro (fresh coriander)

juice of 1 lemon

Ingredients

2 bunches spinach, trimmed and rinsed well

1½ teaspoons ground turmeric

2 tablespoons water

3 tablespoons vegetable oil and melted unsalted butter combined

4 teaspoons cumin seeds

3 yellow (brown) onions, chopped

½ teaspoon salt

2 tablespoons coriander seeds, crushed

1½ tablespoons grated fresh ginger

2 fresh green chili peppers, finely chopped

1 teaspoon chili powder

3 tomatoes, unpeeled, finely chopped

1 recipe Paneer (page 70), cut into 1-inch (2.5-cm) pieces

1 teaspoon dried fenugreek leaves

Chappati (page 98) for serving

Homemade cottage cheese **with spinach**

Palak paneer

Place spinach in a large saucepan. In a small bowl, combine ½ teaspoon turmeric with water and add to pan. Cook over medium–high heat, covered, turning spinach occasionally, until spinach is wilted, 3–5 minutes. Remove from heat, drain excess water and let spinach cool. Place spinach in a food processor or blender and puree. Set aside.

In a karhai or wok, heat oil and butter mixture over medium–low heat. Add cumin seeds and cook until fragrant, about 30 seconds. Add onions and salt, and cook uncovered, stirring often, until onions are translucent, about 5 minutes.

Add coriander seeds, ginger, chili pepper, chili powder and remaining 1 teaspoon turmeric, and cook, stirring, until fragrant, 2–3 minutes.

Stir in tomatoes and cook, stirring occasionally, until tomatoes are soft, about 5 minutes. Stir in pureed spinach and mix well. Add paneer and stir gently to coat with sauce. Cook over medium–low heat until paneer is warmed through, 2–3 minutes. Sprinkle with fenugreek leaves and serve hot with chappati.

Serves 10 as part of an Indian meal

Note: Adding turmeric to spinach before cooking helps spinach to retain a bright green color.

Ingredients

3½ cups (16 oz/660 g) medium to coarse rice flour

1¼ cups (5 oz/150 g) split black lentil flour

salt as needed

cold water as needed

½ cup vegetable oil and melted unsalted butter combined

rice pancakes
Dosai

In a bowl, combine ⅓ cup (2 oz/60 g) rice flour with 2 tablespoons (⅔ oz/20 g) lentil flour and a pinch salt. Make a well in center. Stir in enough cold water to form a batter with a dropping consistency. Cover and let stand in a warm place for 12 hours or overnight.

The next day, in a clean bowl, combine ⅓ cup (2 oz/60 g) rice flour with 2 tablespoons (⅔ oz/20 g) lentil flour and a pinch salt. Make a well in center. Stir in enough cold water to form a batter with a dropping consistency. Stir 1 heaping tablespoon of previous day's batter into new batter. Discard remainder of old batter. Cover new batter and let stand in a warm place for 12 hours or overnight.

1. The next day, in a large clean bowl, combine remaining rice flour with remaining lentil flour and 1 teaspoon salt. Stir in enough cold water to form a new batter with a soft dropping consistency. Stir 1 heaping tablespoon of previous day's batter into new batter. Discard old batter. Cover new batter and let stand in a warm place for 12 hours or overnight. By this stage, the batter should have increased in volume by about half.

2. To cook pancakes: Heat a tawa or heavy griddle over high heat and spread a layer of salt over top. Heat for 3–4 minutes and then, using a clean kitchen towel, wipe off salt. This seasons the pan.

To test if pan is right temperature for cooking pancakes, heat pan over medium heat for 2 minutes. Drizzle lightly with oil and butter mixture, and sprinkle with water. If water sizzles immediately on contact, pan is ready. Wipe pan clean.

3. Use a flat-bottomed metal cup to ladle ⅓ cup (2½ fl oz/80 ml) batter at a time onto pan. Use bottom of cup to spread batter outwards, moving cup in concentric circles. Each pancake should be about 7–8 inches (18–20 cm) in diameter.

4. Drizzle pancake with 1 teaspoon oil and butter mixture and cook until crisp and golden underneath, 2–4 minutes. Place filling along center and roll or fold as desired. Place, seam-side down, on a plate. Repeat with remaining batter and oil and butter mixture.

Makes 10–12 pancakes

Note: For best results, start recipe 3 days before serving.

Ingredients

SAMBHAR (Lentil gravy)

1½ cups (10 oz/300 g) split yellow lentils, rinsed and drained

8 cups (64 fl oz/2 L) water

1 teaspoon ground turmeric

1 lb (500 g) tomatoes, (about 3–4 medium), unpeeled, chopped

2 yellow (brown) onions, chopped

3 tablespoons Sambhar Masala (page 30)

2 teaspoons tamarind concentrate

18 fresh curry leaves

salt to taste

⅔ cup (1 oz/30 g) chopped fresh cilantro (fresh coriander)

POTATO PALLYA (filling)

2 tablespoons vegetable oil

1½ teaspoons brown or black mustard seeds

1 tablespoon split chickpeas (garbanzo beans)

1 tablespoon split black lentils

4 dried red chili peppers

¼ teaspoon powdered asafoetida

2½ teaspoons ground turmeric

18 fresh curry leaves

2 yellow (brown) onions, halved and thinly sliced

½ teaspoon salt, plus extra salt to taste

2 lb (1 kg) cooked desiree or pontiac potatoes, (about 7 medium), peeled and coarsely mashed

½ cup (1 oz/30 g) chopped fresh cilantro (fresh coriander)

1 recipe Dosai (page 74)

Fresh Coconut Chutney (page 102), for serving

Rice and lentil pancakes **with potato filling**

Masala dosai

To make Sambhar: In a large saucepan, combine lentils, water and turmeric, and bring to a boil. Reduce heat to low and cook, partially covered, until lentils are soft and mushy, about 30 minutes. Add tomatoes and onions, and cook, partially covered, stirring occasionally, until soft, about 30 minutes. Add sambhar masala, tamarind, curry leaves and salt, and bring to a boil. Taste and adjust seasoning. Stir in cilantro. Partially cover and keep warm over low heat until serving.

To make Potato Pallya: In a heavy saucepan, heat oil over medium–low heat. Add mustard seeds and cook until they crackle, about 30 seconds. Add chickpeas and lentils and cook over low heat, stirring, until light golden, about 30 seconds; be careful not to burn them. Add chili peppers and asafoetida and cook, stirring, for 15 seconds. Add turmeric and curry leaves, and cook, stirring, for 15 seconds. Stir in onions and ½ teaspoon salt, and cook, stirring often, until onions are translucent, about 5 minutes. Add potatoes and cilantro, and cook, stirring, until well combined, 2–3 minutes. Taste and adjust seasoning if necessary. Cover to keep warm and set aside until serving.

Cook dosai following directions on page 74. Spoon one-tenth of potato filling onto each dosai, fold in sides and place on a serving plate, seam-side down. Serve immediately with sambhar and chutney.

Makes 10–12 filled pancakes

Note: Cook pancakes one at a time unless you have a large, heavy griddle. You will need to cook pancakes just before serving. You can make sambhar 3 days ahead, fresh coconut chutney 1 day ahead, and potato pallya 6 hours ahead.

Ingredients

½ cup (3½ oz/105 g) black lentils, rinsed and drained

½ cup (2 oz/60 g) dried red kidney beans, rinsed and drained

¼ cup (2 oz/60 g) split chickpeas (garbanzo beans), rinsed and drained

5 cups (40 fl oz/1.25 L) water

2½-inch (6-cm) cinnamon stick

3 green cardamom pods, cracked

3 whole cloves

1½ tablespoons finely grated fresh ginger

1½ tablespoons crushed garlic

2–4 teaspoons chili powder

14 oz (440 g) canned crushed peeled tomatoes

⅔ cup (5 oz/150 g) unsalted butter, chopped

salt to taste

4 teaspoons dried fenugreek leaves, crushed

Steamed Basmati Rice (page 92) or Paratha (page 101), for serving

Three lentil broth
Dal makhani

Place lentils, kidney beans, chickpeas and water in a large bowl. Cover and let stand overnight.

The next day, place lentil mixture and liquid in a large, heavy saucepan. Place cinnamon, cardamom and cloves in a square of cheesecloth (muslin), bring up the corners to form a bundle, tie with kitchen twine, and add to pan. Bring to a boil. Reduce heat to low and cook, uncovered, until lentils, beans and chickpeas are tender, about 1½ hours. Add extra water if necessary to keep lentil mixture covered.

Remove bundle of spices and discard. Add ginger, garlic, chili powder, tomatoes, butter and salt to pan. Raise heat to medium and cook, stirring often, for 10 minutes. The consistency should be like thick soup. If too thick, add a small amount of water. Taste and adjust seasoning. Stir in fenugreek leaves. Serve hot with rice or paratha.

Serves 10 as part of an Indian meal

Creamy lentil and **split-pea dal**

Moong matar dhaniwal

Place lentils and split peas in a bowl and add cold water to cover. Set aside for 30 minutes. Drain.

Fill a large saucepan with water and bring to a boil. Add lentils, split peas, turmeric and chili pepper. Boil, uncovered, until lentils and peas are tender, about 30 minutes. Drain, place in a bowl and mash coarsely. Set aside.

In a saucepan, heat oil over medium–low heat and add mustard seeds. Cook until they crackle, about 30 seconds. Stir in cumin seeds and cook until aromatic, about 30 seconds. Stir in garam masala and coriander. Stir in mashed lentils and peas, water, cream and tomato. Season with salt. Bring to a boil over medium heat, reduce heat to low and simmer, partially covered, stirring often, for 4 minutes. Adjust seasoning. Stir in cilantro and serve hot.

Serves 6–8 as part of an Indian meal

Ingredients

²/₃ cup (5 oz/150 g) lentils, rinsed and drained

²/₃ cup (5 oz/150 g) yellow split peas, rinsed and drained

1 teaspoon ground turmeric

2 fresh green chili peppers, halved lengthwise

4 teaspoons vegetable oil

1 teaspoon brown or black mustard seeds

1 teaspoon cumin seeds

2 teaspoons Garam Masala (page 28)

1 teaspoon ground coriander

½ cup (4 fl oz/125 ml) water

3 tablespoons heavy (double) cream

1 large tomato, unpeeled, chopped

salt to taste

¼ cup (⅓ oz/10 g) chopped fresh cilantro (fresh coriander)

Eggs poached on tomato

Tamatar kothmir per eeda

In a large, wide, heavy frying pan, heat oil and butter mixture over medium–low heat. Add onions and salt, and cook uncovered, stirring often, until onions are golden brown, 10–15 minutes.

Add ginger and garlic, and cook, stirring, for 1 minute. Add turmeric and cook, stirring, for 30 seconds. Stir in tomatoes and chili pepper, and cook uncovered, stirring often, until tomatoes are soft, about 5 minutes. Add cilantro and mix well.

Spread tomato mixture evenly in pan and use a spoon to make eight evenly spaced indentations in mixture. Break an egg into each indentation, cover pan and cook over low heat until eggs are just set, about 10 minutes. Serve hot.

Serves 8 as part of an Indian meal

Note: This dish is excellent for breakfast or brunch, served with toast or bread rolls.

Ingredients

- ⅓ cup (3 fl oz/90 ml) vegetable oil and melted unsalted butter combined
- 3 yellow (brown) onions, finely chopped
- ½ teaspoon salt
- 1½ tablespoons finely chopped fresh ginger
- 6 cloves garlic, finely chopped
- ½ teaspoon ground turmeric
- 2 lb (1 kg) tomatoes, (about 7 medium), unpeeled, finely chopped
- 3 fresh green chili peppers, finely chopped
- ⅔ cup (1 oz/30 g) chopped fresh cilantro (fresh coriander)
- 8 eggs

Ingredients

1 lb (500 g) pumpkin or butternut squash, peeled and grated

2 large desiree or pontiac potatoes, 10 oz (300g) total, boiled, peeled and mashed

¼ cup (⅓ oz/10 g) chopped fresh cilantro (fresh coriander)

1 tablespoon finely grated fresh ginger

3 teaspoons finely chopped fresh green chili peppers

salt to taste

SAUCE

¼ cup (2 fl oz/60 ml) vegetable oil

1-inch (2.5-cm) cinnamon stick

4 green cardamom pods

4 whole cloves

1 small yellow (brown) onion, halved and thinly sliced

½ teaspoon salt, plus extra salt to taste

1 tablespoon finely grated fresh ginger

1 tablespoon crushed garlic

3 teaspoons ground turmeric

2 teaspoons chili powder

2 tomatoes, unpeeled, chopped

1 teaspoon honey

1 teaspoon ground mace

cornstarch (cornflour) for dusting

vegetable oil for deep-frying

3–4 tablespoons heavy (double) cream

½ teaspoon Garam Masala (page 28)

VEGETABLES

Pumpkin dumplings in malai sauce
Kaddu kofta

Place grated pumpkin or squash in a colander and squeeze well to extract any excess water. Place in a bowl with potatoes, cilantro, ginger and chili pepper. Season with salt and mix well. Set aside.

To make sauce: In a karhai or frying pan, heat oil over medium–low heat. Add cinnamon, cardamom and cloves, and cook until fragrant, about 30 seconds. Add onion and ½ teaspoon salt, and cook uncovered, stirring often, until onion is dark golden brown, 10–15 minutes. Stir in ginger and garlic, and cook for 30 seconds. Add turmeric and chili powder, and cook, stirring, for 30 seconds. Stir in tomatoes and cook, stirring, until tomatoes soften, 3–4 minutes. Stir in honey and mace. Cover to keep warm.

Meanwhile, shape pumpkin mixture into walnut-sized balls, dust with cornstarch and place on a baking sheet dusted with cornstarch.

Fill a medium saucepan with oil to a depth of 3 inches (7.5 cm). Heat oil over medium–high heat to 375°F (190°C) on a deep-frying thermometer. Carefully add dumplings in batches of five and cook until golden brown, 2–3 minutes. Remove with a slotted spoon and drain on paper towels.

Place dumplings on a serving dish. Stir cream into sauce and pour over dumplings. Sprinkle with garam masala, season with extra salt to taste, and serve hot.

Serves 8–10 as part of an Indian meal

Note: Dumplings are best shaped and cooked close to serving time. The mixture can be made 2 hours ahead and kept at room temperature.

Cumin-flavored potatoes

Jeera aloo

Place potatoes and large pinch salt in a saucepan with enough cold water to cover. Bring to a boil over medium–high heat. Reduce heat to medium–low and cook, partially covered, until potatoes are tender, about 20 minutes. Drain potatoes and let cool for 15 minutes. Peel potatoes and cut into 1½-inch (4-cm) cubes. Set aside.

In a small bowl, combine cold water, turmeric and chili powder, and set aside.

In a large, heavy saucepan, heat oil and butter mixture over medium–low heat. Add cumin seeds and cook, stirring, until fragrant, about 30 seconds; take care not to burn seeds. Reduce heat to low and add water and turmeric mixture. Cook, stirring, for 30 seconds. Add potatoes and salt to taste, and toss gently until heated through, about 1 minute. Add coriander and toss for 30 seconds. Add ginger and cilantro and toss to combine. Drizzle with lemon juice and serve.

Serves 8–10 as part of an Indian meal

Ingredients

2 lb (1 kg) uniformly sized desiree or pontiac potatoes, (about 7 medium)

salt as needed

2½ tablespoons cold water

1 teaspoon ground turmeric

½ teaspoon chili powder

¼ cup (2 fl oz/60 ml) vegetable oil and melted unsalted butter combined

4 teaspoons cumin seeds

4 teaspoons ground coriander

2 teaspoons finely grated fresh ginger

⅓ cup (½ oz/15 g) chopped fresh cilantro (fresh coriander)

juice of ½ lemon

Ingredients

2 lb (1 kg) green beans, trimmed and cut into ½-inch (12-mm) pieces

1½ teaspoons ground turmeric

2½ tablespoons vegetable oil

1 teaspoon brown or black mustard seeds

5 dried red chili peppers

18 fresh curry leaves

1 tablespoon finely grated fresh ginger

2 yellow (brown) onions, chopped

½ teaspoon salt

4 fresh green chili peppers, chopped

½ cup (2 oz/60 g) finely grated fresh coconut

juice of ½ lemon

Beans **foogarth**

Fill a saucepan with water and bring to a boil. Add beans and ½ teaspoon turmeric and boil for 1–2 minutes. Drain and rinse beans under cold running water. Drain well.

In a karhai or wok, heat oil over medium–low heat. Add mustard seeds and cook until they crackle, about 30 seconds. Add dried chili peppers, curry leaves and ginger, and cook, stirring, for 30 seconds. Add onions, remaining 1 teaspoon turmeric and salt. Cook, uncovered, stirring often, until onions are translucent, about 5 minutes.

Stir in beans and fresh chili pepper, and toss over medium–low heat until well combined and heated through. Sprinkle with coconut and drizzle with lemon juice. Serve hot.

Serves 10 as part of an Indian meal

Note: The addition of turmeric when cooking beans helps to intensify the green color of the beans.

Sweet-and-sour potatoes

Khate meethe aloo

Place potatoes and large pinch salt in a saucepan with enough cold water to cover. Bring to a boil over medium–high heat. Reduce heat to medium–low and cook, partially covered, until potatoes are tender, about 20 minutes. Drain potatoes and let cool for 15 minutes. Peel potatoes and cut into 1½-inch (4-cm) cubes. Set aside.

In a karhai or wok, heat oil over medium–low heat. Add mustard seeds and cook until they crackle, about 30 seconds. Add curry leaves and turmeric, and cook, stirring, for 15 seconds. Add potatoes and season with salt. Toss gently to combine. Add coconut milk, cilantro, chili pepper and sugar, and simmer, gently stirring occasionally, for 2 minutes. Drizzle with lemon juice and serve hot.

Serves 8 as part of an Indian meal

Ingredients

1 lb (500 g) uniformly sized desiree or pontiac potatoes, (about 3–4 medium)

salt as needed

3 tablespoons vegetable oil

½ teaspoon brown or black mustard seeds

36 fresh curry leaves

½ teaspoon ground turmeric

½ cup (4 fl oz/125 ml) coconut milk

¼ cup (⅓ oz/10 g) chopped fresh cilantro (fresh coriander)

4 teaspoons finely chopped fresh green chili peppers

1 teaspoon sugar

juice of 1 lemon

Ingredients

2 ears (cobs) of corn

2 teaspoons unsalted butter

3 tablespoons vegetable oil

½-inch (12-mm) cinnamon stick

2 green cardamom pods

2 whole cloves

2 yellow (brown) onions, chopped

½ teaspoon salt, plus extra salt to taste

1 teaspoon finely grated fresh ginger

1 teaspoon crushed garlic

1 teaspoon chili powder

1 tablespoon coriander seeds, crushed

1 teaspoon ground turmeric

1 large tomato, unpeeled, finely chopped

1 lb (500 g) small button mushrooms, wiped clean

juice of ½ lemon

¼ cup (⅓ oz/10 g) chopped fresh cilantro (fresh coriander)

Mushrooms and corn with **cilantro**
Khumb makki hara dhania

Use a sharp knife to remove kernels from ears of corn. In a large saucepan, melt butter over medium–high heat. Add corn and cook, stirring, until softened, 2–3 minutes. Remove to a small bowl and set aside.

In same pan, heat oil over medium–low heat. Add cinnamon, cardamom and cloves, and cook, stirring, until fragrant, about 30 seconds. Add onions and ½ teaspoon salt, and cook, uncovered, stirring often, until onions are dark golden brown, 10–15 minutes.

Add ginger and garlic, and cook, stirring, for 30 seconds. Add chili powder, coriander and turmeric, and cook, stirring, until fragrant, about 30 seconds. Add tomato and cook, stirring often, until tomato is soft, about 5 minutes. Add mushrooms and corn, and cook, tossing occasionally, until mushrooms are slightly soft, 5–10 minutes. Add lemon juice and add salt to taste if necessary. Add cilantro and toss gently. Serve hot.

Serves 8–10 as part of an Indian meal

Ingredients

1 large yellow (brown) onion, finely chopped

1 English (hothouse) cucumber, coarsely grated

1 carrot, peeled and coarsely grated

2 fresh green chili peppers, chopped

½ cup (½ oz/15 g) chopped fresh cilantro (fresh coriander)

1 tablespoon finely chopped fresh ginger

⅓ cup (2 oz/60 g) roasted unsalted peanuts, finely chopped

1 teaspoon ground white pepper

salt to taste

juice of 1 lemon

Ingredients

8 cups (64 fl oz/2 L) water

1½ cups (10 oz/300 g) split yellow lentils, rinsed and drained

1½ cups (3 oz/90 g) cauliflower florets

4 oz (125 g) green beans, cut into 1-inch (2.5-cm) pieces

1 carrot, peeled and cut into 1-inch (2.5-cm) sticks

⅓ cup (2 oz/60 g) shelled fresh or frozen green peas

2 teaspoons ground turmeric

salt to taste

⅓ cup (3 fl oz/90 ml) vegetable oil

4 teaspoons brown or black mustard seeds

1 teaspoon powdered asafoetida

1 tablespoon finely grated fresh ginger

1 tablespoon crushed garlic

1 teaspoon chili powder

18 fresh curry leaves

juice of 1 lemon

½ cup (¾ oz/20 g) chopped fresh cilantro (fresh coriander)

Shredded mixed vegetable salad

Koshumbir

In a glass or ceramic bowl, combine all ingredients and mix well. Serve chilled.

Serves 8–10 as part of an Indian meal

Note: Salad can be made up to 1 day ahead.

Mixed vegetables with lentils

Subz dal tadka

Place water, lentils, cauliflower, beans, carrot, peas and 1 teaspoon turmeric in a large, heavy saucepan. Bring to a simmer over medium heat, reduce heat to low and cook, partially covered, until lentils are soft and mushy, about 1 hour. Season well with salt and set aside.

In a small, heavy saucepan, heat oil over low heat. Add mustard seeds and cook until they crackle, about 30 seconds. Add asafoetida and stir for 5 seconds. Add ginger and garlic, and cook, stirring, for 30 seconds; take care not to burn mixture. Add remaining 1 teaspoon turmeric, chili powder and curry leaves, and cook, stirring, for 5 seconds.

Pour mixture over lentils, cover and set aside for 5 minutes. Stir in lemon juice and sprinkle with cilantro leaves. Serve hot.

Serves 10 as part of an Indian meal

Vegetables in spiced yoghurt

Vegetable khurma

In a large saucepan, combine water, chili pepper, curry leaves and turmeric and bring to a boil over medium–high heat. Add potato, carrot, onion, eggplant, zucchini and beans, and mix well. Cover, reduce heat to medium–low and simmer, stirring occasionally, until vegetables are just tender, about 15 minutes.

While vegetables cook, make spiced yogurt. In a bowl, combine yogurt, coriander, cumin, pepper and salt, and mix well.

Drain all but about 1½ tablespoons liquid from vegetables. Add spiced yogurt and mix gently over very low heat until combined. Do not overheat or yogurt may separate. Serve hot.

Serves 8–10 as part of an Indian meal

Ingredients

1¼ cups (10 fl oz/300 ml) water

4 large fresh green chili peppers, quartered lengthwise

18 fresh curry leaves

½ teaspoon ground turmeric

1 large desiree potato, cut into 2-inch (5-cm) sticks

1 large carrot, cut into 2-inch (5-cm) sticks

1 yellow (brown) onion, cut into very thin wedges

1 baby eggplant (aubergine), cut into 2-inch (5-cm) sticks

1 large zucchini (courgette), cut into 2-inch (5-cm) sticks

4 oz (125 g) green beans, trimmed and cut into 2-inch (5-cm) lengths

SPICED YOGURT

½ cup (4 oz/125 g) plain (natural) whole-milk yogurt

½ teaspoon ground coriander

½ teaspoon ground cumin

¼ teaspoon ground black pepper

salt to taste

Ingredients

2½ cups (1 lb/500 g) basmati rice

5 cups (40 fl oz/1.2 L) water

½ teaspoon salt

Steamed **basmati rice**

Place rice in a bowl and add cold water to cover. Swirl with your hand, let rice settle, then drain off water. Repeat six or seven times. Add 5 cups (40 fl oz/1.2 L) water to rice and set aside to soak for 20 minutes.

Drain water from rice into a large, heavy saucepan with a tight-fitting lid. Add salt and bring to a boil over medium–high heat. Add soaked rice, stir once, then bring to a boil. Reduce heat to low and cook, partially covered, until most of water is absorbed and steam holes appear in rice, 10–15 minutes.

Cover and reduce heat to very low. Let rice steam for 10 minutes without lifting lid. Remove from heat and set aside for 5–10 minutes without lifting lid. Fluff grains with a fork and serve.

Serves 8–10

Note: You can easily halve or double this recipe. It's important to rinse rice well before cooking to remove excess starch; otherwise rice can become gluey. A general guide is to soak rice in twice its volume of water then cook it in soaking water. The rice must be steamed over very low heat for last 10 minutes of cooking. Use a heat diffuser if you have one, or place saucepan on a wok stand over heat source.

Tomato **rice**

Place rice in a bowl and add cold water to cover. Swirl rice with your hand, let rice settle, then drain off water. Repeat six or seven times. Cover rice with water and set aside to soak for 20 minutes.

In a large saucepan, bring 3 qt (3 L) water to a boil. Drain rice and add to pan with ½ teaspoon salt. Bring to a boil and cook, uncovered, until rice is just cooked, 9–10 minutes. Do not overcook. Drain in a colander and set aside.

In a large saucepan, heat oil over medium–low heat. Add mustard seeds and cook until they crackle, about 30 seconds. Add chickpeas and lentils and cook, stirring, until light golden, 1–2 minutes. Add chili powder, turmeric and asafoetida, and cook, stirring, for 15 seconds. Add ginger and curry leaves, and mix well. Add tomatoes, raise heat to medium and cook, stirring often, until tomatoes are soft and mixture thickens slightly, 15–20 minutes.

Taste and add salt if necessary. Add drained rice and toss gently with a large spoon to combine rice and tomatoes, taking care not to crush rice. Sprinkle with cilantro and serve.

Serves 10

Note: Rice is best cooked close to serving. Tomato mixture can be made several hours ahead; reheat before adding rice.

Ingredients

2½ cups (1 lb/500 g) basmati rice

3 qt (3 L) water

½ teaspoon salt, plus extra salt to taste

⅓ cup (3 fl oz/90 ml) vegetable oil

4 teaspoons brown or black mustard seeds

4 teaspoons split chickpeas (garbanzo beans)

1 teaspoon split black lentils

2 teaspoons chili powder

1 teaspoon ground turmeric

½ teaspoon powdered asafoetida

1½ tablespoons finely grated fresh ginger

18 fresh curry leaves

2 lb (1 kg) tomatoes, (about 7 medium), unpeeled, finely chopped

⅓ cup (½ oz/15 g) chopped fresh cilantro (fresh coriander)

Ingredients

2½ cups (1 lb/500 g) basmati rice

⅓ cup (3 fl oz/90 ml) vegetable oil and melted unsalted butter combined

¾-inch (2-cm) cinnamon stick

1 brown or black cardamom pod

2 green cardamom pods

2 whole cloves

½ mace blade

2 yellow (brown) onions, halved and thinly sliced

about 1 teaspoon salt

1 tablespoon finely grated fresh ginger

1 tablespoon crushed garlic

2 tomatoes, unpeeled, finely chopped

1 carrot, cut into 1-inch (2.5-cm) sticks

4 oz (125 g) green beans, trimmed and cut into 1-inch (2.5-cm) sticks

½ cup (2½ oz/75 g) shelled fresh or frozen green peas

1½ tablespoons chopped fresh green chili peppers

3¾ cups (30 fl oz/940 ml) vegetable stock or water

½ cup (¾ oz/25 g) chopped fresh cilantro (fresh coriander)

Vegetable **pulao**

Place rice in a bowl and add cold water to cover. Swirl rice with your hand, let rice settle, then drain off water. Repeat six or seven times. Cover rice with water and set aside to soak for 20 minutes.

Preheat oven to 350°F (180°C/Gas 4).

In a large, heavy deghchi or ovenproof saucepan, heat oil and butter mixture over low heat. Add cinnamon, cardamom, cloves and mace, and cook, stirring, until fragrant, about 30 seconds. Add onions and salt, and cook, uncovered, stirring occasionally, until onions are dark golden brown, about 15 minutes. Add ginger and garlic, and cook for 30 seconds. Stir in tomatoes and mix well. Stir in carrot, beans, peas and chili pepper, and cook, stirring, for 3 minutes.

Drain rice and add to pan, stirring until well combined. Stir in stock or water and bring to a simmer. Cook, partially covered, until tunnels begin to appear in rice mixture, about 10 minutes.

Cover pan tightly and bake in oven until rice is tender, about 15 minutes. Remove from oven and let stand for 10 minutes. Garnish with cilantro and serve immediately.

Serves 8 as part of an Indian meal

Note: The recipe can be doubled to serve 14–16.

Andhra-style chicken pulao

Preheat oven to 425°F (220°C/Gas 7).

Place rice in a bowl and add cold water to cover. Swirl rice with your hand, let rice settle, then drain off water. Repeat six or seven times. Cover rice with water and set aside to soak for 20 minutes. In another bowl, combine onions with ½ teaspoon salt and set aside.

In a heavy deghchi or saucepan about 12 inches (30 cm) in diameter, heat oil and butter mixture over medium–low heat. Add cinnamon, cardamom and cloves, and cook until fragrant, about 30 seconds. Add star anise and half of curry leaves, and stir well. Add onions to pan and cook, uncovered, stirring often, until onions are dark golden brown, 10–15 minutes.

Add chicken pieces and cook, turning occasionally, until chicken is lightly browned, about 10 minutes. Add ginger, garlic, chili pepper, remaining curry leaves, and buttermilk, and season with salt (not too much if using seasoned stock). Cook, uncovered, turning chicken occasionally, until chicken is cooked through and liquid reduces by half (liquid may look curdled), 10–15 minutes.

Add tomatoes and coconut milk, and cook, stirring often, until tomatoes are slightly soft, about 5 minutes. Add stock or water and mix well. Bring to a boil over medium–high heat. Drain rice, add to pan and mix well. Cook, partially covered, until most of liquid is absorbed and steam holes appear in mixture, about 10 minutes.

Remove from heat and cover pan with a wet, clean kitchen towel. Cover tightly with lid, compressing towel around edge of pan. Bake in oven for 20 minutes. Remove from oven and set aside for 10 minutes. Sprinkle with cilantro and serve hot accompanied by lemon wedges.

Serves 10–12 as part of an Indian meal

Ingredients

5 cups (2 lb/1 kg) basmati rice

3 large yellow (brown) onions, halved and thinly sliced

½ teaspoon salt, plus extra salt to taste

7 fl oz (210 ml) vegetable oil and melted unsalted butter combined

1½-inch (4-cm) cinnamon stick

2 green cardamom pods

3 whole cloves

2 star anise

36 fresh curry leaves

2½ lb (1.5 kg) chicken pieces or 1 whole 2½-lb (1.5 kg) chicken cut into 16 pieces

1 tablespoon finely grated fresh ginger

1 tablespoon crushed garlic

5 fresh green chili peppers, sliced lengthwise

1⅔ cups (13 fl oz/400 ml) buttermilk

4 tomatoes, finely chopped

7 fl oz (210 ml) canned coconut milk

5 cups (40 fl oz/1.2 L) chicken stock or water

1 cup (1½ oz/45 g) chopped fresh cilantro (fresh coriander)

1 lemon, cut into wedges, for serving

Chappati
(Flat bread)

Ingredients

5 cups (1½ lb/750 g) whole wheat (wholemeal) flour

1 teaspoon salt

3 tablespoons vegetable oil

about 2 cups (16 fl oz/500 ml) water

vegetable oil and melted unsalted butter combined, for brushing

Sift flour and salt into a large mixing bowl. Make a well in center. Add oil and enough water, adding water in increments, to form a soft dough with your hand. Knead dough lightly in bowl, cover with a clean damp kitchen towel, and set aside for 20 minutes.

Turn out dough onto a lightly floured surface and knead until it almost springs back when touched lightly, about 10 minutes. Cover with damp towel and set aside for 15 minutes. Knead dough lightly and divide evenly into 12 portions. Shape each portion into a ball, then roll out into a disk 8–10 inches (20–25 cm) in diameter.

Heat a heavy cast-iron griddle over medium heat. When griddle is hot, place a disk of dough on griddle and cook, lightly pressing disk all over with a dry clean kitchen towel, using a dabbing motion, until disk is golden brown in spots, 1–2 minutes. Turn and cook on second side until golden brown in spots and cooked through, about 1 minute. Brush with oil and butter mixture and remove to a serving tray lined with a cloth napkin. Repeat with remaining disks.

Makes 12 chappati

Note: The griddle must not be too hot or chappati will become dry and burnt. You can also make chappati smaller if you prefer. Chappati can be cooked several hours ahead. Before serving, wrap them in a clean kitchen towel, then aluminum foil, and heat in an oven preheated to 225°F (110°C/Gas ¼) for 5–10 minutes.

Poori
(Puffed fried bread)

Ingredients

5 cups (1½ lb/750 g) whole wheat (wholemeal) flour

1 teaspoon salt

5 tablespoons vegetable oil

2 cups (16 fl oz/500 ml) water

8 cups (64 fl oz/2 L) vegetable oil for deep-frying

Sift flour and salt into a large bowl. Make a well in center. Add oil and water, and mix with your hands to form a firm dough. Knead dough on a lightly floured work surface until it almost springs back when touched lightly, about 10 minutes. Cover with a damp clean kitchen towel and set aside for 20 minutes.

Turn out dough onto a floured work surface and knead lightly. Divide evenly into 50 portions. Roll each portion into a ball, then roll out into a disk 4–6 inches (10–15 cm) in diameter. Lightly dust each disk with flour. Set disks on a baking sheet, partially overlapping them.

In large saucepan, heat oil over medium heat to 375°F (190°C) on a deep-frying thermometer. Carefully slide a disk in oil and keep submerged with a slotted spoon until disk puffs well, rises to surface of oil and is golden brown underneath, 30–60 seconds. Gently turn disk without piercing surface and cook second side until golden brown. Remove to paper towels to drain. Repeat with remaining disks.

Makes 50 poori; serves about 10

Note: Poori are best cooked just before serving but dough can be rolled several hours in advance. Dust with flour and cover with a damp kitchen towel to keep moist.

Step-by-step **paratha**
(Flaky flat bread)

Ingredients

5⅓ cups (26½ oz/800 g) all-purpose (plain) flour, plus flour for dusting

1⅓ cups (6½ oz/200 g) whole wheat (wholemeal) flour

¼ teaspoon baking soda

a pinch cream of tartar

2 teaspoons sugar

1½ teaspoons salt

1 teaspoon nigella seeds

1 egg

6 tablespoons vegetable oil

1¾ cups (14 fl oz/430 ml) buttermilk

about ⅓ cup (3 fl oz/90 ml) water

2 oz (60 g) melted unsalted butter for brushing

Sift flours, baking soda and cream of tartar into a large mixing bowl. Stir in sugar, salt and nigella seeds. Make a well in center.

In a small bowl, whisk together egg and oil, and add to well. Using a wooden spoon or fingers, gradually mix flour into egg mixture, adding buttermilk and enough water to form a soft dough. Knead dough for 10 minutes. Cover with a damp clean kitchen towel and set aside for 15 minutes. Knead for 5 minutes, cover, and set aside for 10 minutes.

1. Knead dough for 1 minute, then divide evenly into 24 portions. Roll each portion into a ball, dust lightly with flour and cover with a clean kitchen towel.

2. Roll out each ball on a lightly floured work surface into a disk 7 inches (18 cm) in diameter. Brush lightly with melted butter and dust very lightly with flour. Fold in half. Brush with butter and dust with flour, and fold in half again. Dust lightly with flour, set aside in a single layer, and cover with a clean kitchen towel while rolling remaining balls.

Roll out each folded portion of dough into a triangle shape about ⅛-inch (3-mm) thick.

3. Heat a tawa or heavy griddle over medium heat. Place a triangle of dough on surface and cook, lightly pressing all over with a dry clean kitchen towel, or metal spatula until browned, 2–3 minutes. Turn and cook on second side, and lightly brush cooked side with butter. Turn again and cook on first side for 30 seconds, lightly brushing exposed side with butter. Turn again and cook for 30 seconds on second side.

Makes 24 paratha

Note: Paratha can be rolled about 30 minutes before cooking. Keep covered at room temperature.

Ingredients

1 whole fresh coconut

½ cup (¾ oz/20 g) coarsely chopped fresh cilantro (fresh coriander) leaves and stems

2 fresh green chili peppers, coarsely chopped

2½ teaspoons finely grated fresh ginger

salt to taste

3–4 tablespoons cold water

2 teaspoons vegetable oil

1½ teaspoons brown or black mustard seeds

½ teaspoon powdered asafoetida

18 fresh curry leaves, coarsely chopped

1

2

3

Step-by-step fresh coconut chutney

To open coconut, carefully pierce "eyes" of coconut with a thick metal skewer, a screwdriver or other pointed object.

1. Drain coconut water into a cup. Taste coconut water to make sure it is sweet and not off-tasting (keep the water for drinking as it is highly nutritious).

2. Use a hammer to crack coconut open. Turn pieces rounded-side up and use hammer to break them into small pieces about 3 inches (7.5 cm) wide. Use a small, sharp knife to pry coconut meat from shell. Peel tough brown skin from meat.

3. Place meat in a food processor and process until finely chopped. Add cilantro, chili pepper, ginger and salt. Process until all ingredients are finely chopped, adding 3–4 tablespoons water if necessary to facilitate processing. Transfer mixture to a bowl.

In a small saucepan, heat oil over medium heat. Add mustard seeds and cook, stirring, until they begin to crackle, about 30 seconds. Remove from heat and quickly stir in asafoetida and curry leaves, mixing well.

Add mustard seed mixture to coconut chutney and mix well. Taste and add salt if necessary.

Serves 8

Note: Chutney can be made 1 day ahead. Store in an airtight container in refrigerator.

Date and tamarind chutney

Ingredients

2 lb (1 kg) pitted, dried dates

3 cups (24 fl oz/750 ml) white vinegar

8 oz (250 g) jaggery or dark brown sugar

¾ cup (6 oz/180 g) salt

1 cup (8 fl oz/250 ml) vegetable oil

⅓ cup (3½ oz/105 g) tamarind concentrate

⅔ cup (3 oz/90 g) chili powder

5 x 3-inch (7.5-cm) cinnamon sticks, broken into 1-inch (2.5-cm) pieces

2½ tablespoons green cardamom pods

3 tablespoons whole cloves

4 teaspoons chat masala

In a large, heavy saucepan, combine dates, vinegar, jaggery or brown sugar, salt, oil, tamarind, chili powder, cinnamon, cardamom and cloves. Cook over medium heat, stirring, until mixture begins to bubble. Reduce heat to low and cook, partially covered and stirring often, until dates are soft, 35–45 minutes.

Remove from heat, add chat masala and mix well. Spoon hot chutney into clean glass jars and immediately seal with lids. Turn jars upside-down and set aside for 5 minutes. Turn upright and set aside to cool. Label with name and date. Store in a cool cupboard for at least 1 week before opening.

Makes about 6 cups (48 fl oz/1.5 L)

Note: Unopened chutney will keep for up to 1 year in a cool, dark cupboard. After opening, keep in refrigerator for up to 6 months. The chutney sterilizes the jars and lids because the jars are filled, sealed and inverted while chutney is boiling hot.

Herb and ginger yogurt dip (churri)

Ingredients

1 teaspoon cumin seeds

½ cup (¾ oz/20 g) coarsely chopped fresh mint

½ cup (¾ oz/20 g) coarsely chopped fresh cilantro (fresh coriander)

2 teaspoons finely chopped fresh ginger

2 fresh green chili peppers, coarsely chopped

2½ cups (20 oz/600 g) plain (natural) whole-milk yogurt

1 yellow (brown) onion, halved and thinly sliced

salt to taste

In a small saucepan over low heat, dry-roast cumin seeds until fragrant and lightly colored, being careful not to burn. Let cool then grind to a powder in a spice grinder.

Place mint, cilantro, ginger and chili pepper in a food processor and process until finely chopped.

In a bowl, whisk yogurt. Add onion, ground cumin and chopped herb mixture. Mix well and season with salt.

Serves 8–10 as an accompaniment

Note: Churri can be made 2 days ahead. Store in an airtight container in refrigerator.

Carrot with yogurt and spices (carrot pachadi)

Ingredients

2 cups (1 lb/500 g) plain (natural) whole-milk yogurt

1 lb (500 g) carrots, (about 4–5 medium), peeled and grated

salt to taste

1½ tablespoons vegetable oil

1 teaspoon black mustard seeds

3 dried red chili peppers

18 fresh curry leaves

¼ teaspoon powdered asafoetida

¼ cup (⅓ oz/10 g) chopped fresh cilantro (fresh coriander)

In a bowl, whisk yogurt. Add carrots and mix well. Season with salt.

In a small saucepan, heat oil over medium–low heat. Add mustard seeds and cook until they crackle, about 30 seconds. Stir in chili peppers, curry leaves and asafoetida, and cook, stirring, for 15 seconds. Add to yogurt and carrot mixture and mix well. Sprinkle with cilantro before serving.

Serves 8–10 as an accompaniment

Note: Carrot pachadi can be made up to 6 hours ahead. Store in an airtight container in refrigerator.

Mint and **yogurt dip** (mint raita)

Ingredients

½ **cup (¾ oz/20 g) coarsely chopped fresh mint**

½ **cup (¾ oz/20 g) coarsely chopped fresh cilantro (fresh coriander)**

4 **teaspoons finely grated fresh ginger**

2 **teaspoons finely chopped fresh green chili peppers**

1 **cup (8 oz/250 g) plain (natural) whole-milk yogurt**

salt to taste

Place mint, cilantro, ginger and chili pepper in a food processor and process until finely chopped.

In a bowl, whisk yogurt. Add chopped mint mixture and mix well. Season with salt.

Serves 8

Note: Raitas are based on yogurt, which is whipped or whisked. You can use either whole-milk (full-fat) or reduced-fat yogurt. This raita can be made 1 day ahead. Store in an airtight container in refrigerator.

Cucumber and **yogurt dip** (cucumber raita)

Ingredients

1½ **teaspoons cumin seeds**

1 **cup (8 oz/250 g) plain (natural) whole-milk yogurt**

1 **English (hothouse) cucumber, finely chopped**

salt and freshly ground black pepper to taste

¼ **cup (⅓ oz/10 g) chopped fresh cilantro (fresh coriander)**

In a small saucepan over low heat, dry-roast cumin seeds until fragrant and lightly colored, being careful not to burn them. Let cool then grind to a powder in a spice grinder.

In a bowl, whisk yogurt. Add cucumber and ground cumin, and season with salt and pepper. Mix well. Stir in cilantro and mix well.

Serves 8

Note: This raita can be made up to 6 hours ahead. Store in an airtight container in refrigerator.

Ingredients

15 limes, rinsed and thoroughly dried

1 cup (8 oz/250 g) salt

juice of 4 limes

3 tablespoons vegetable oil

1 teaspoon fenugreek seeds

2 teaspoons ground turmeric

1 teaspoon powdered asafoetida

2/3 cup (3 oz/90 g) chili powder

Step-by-step making lime pickle

1. Rinse and thoroughly dry limes.

2. Cut limes into quarters, then cut each quarter evenly into thirds. In a bowl, combine lime pieces, salt and lime juice. Spoon into a 4-cup (32-fl oz/1-L) capacity airtight glass jar that has been thoroughly washed and dried. Seal jar and set aside at room temperature for 1 week.

3. In a small saucepan or wok, heat oil over medium–low heat. Add fenugreek and cook, stirring, until golden, about 30 seconds. Remove from heat and place seeds in a spice grinder. Add turmeric and asafoetida to oil remaining in pan and cook, stirring, for 30 seconds. Remove from heat. Grind fenugreek to a powder and add to pan.

Pour lime mixture into a large bowl that has been thoroughly washed and dried. Add chili powder and spice mixture, and mix thoroughly.

4. Return lime mixture to jar and seal. Set aside for 2 weeks at room temperature to pickle then store in refrigerator.

Note: The jar and all utensils and bowls must be completely clean and dry. The limes must be completely dry before cutting. Lime pickle will keep for up to 6 months in refrigerator.

1

2

3

4

Ingredients

large pinch saffron threads

½ cup (4 fl oz/125 ml) milk, heated

⅓ cup (3½ oz/105 g) pistachio nuts

3 tablespoons green cardamom pods

1⅔ cups (13 fl oz/400 ml) sweetened condensed milk

3 cups (24 fl oz/750 ml) heavy (double) cream

RICH SAUCE

½ cup (4 oz/125 g) raw or Demarara sugar

½ cup (4 fl oz/125 ml) heavy (double) cream

5 star anise

Saffron and pistachio ice cream
Saffron and pista kulfi

In a bowl, combine saffron and hot milk and set aside for 10 minutes. Place pistachio nuts in a food processor and process until finely chopped. In a spice grinder, grind cardamom to a powder.

Place condensed milk and cream in a bowl. Stir until well combined; do not whisk or beat. Add pistachio nuts, saffron and milk mixture, and ground cardamom. Stir until well combined.

Divide mixture among 10 ramekins with a ½-cup (4-fl oz/125-ml) capacity. Place in freezer until ice cream is frozen, about 6 hours. Cover ramekins well and keep in freezer until serving.

To make sauce: In a saucepan, combine sugar, cream and star anise. Stir over low heat until sugar dissolves. Bring to a boil, reduce heat to low and cook, uncovered, stirring often, until slightly thickened, about 10 minutes.

To serve, briefly dip each ramekin in a bowl of hot water. Invert a serving plate on top and invert plate and ramekin to unmold ice cream. Top with sauce and serve immediately.

Serves 10

Note: You can make ice cream up to 2 weeks ahead. Wrap well to prevent flavors being absorbed from other foods in freezer. Make sauce close to serving.

Mango ice cream

Mango kulfi

Ingredients

- 1 ripe mango, about 12 oz (360 g), peeled, pitted and coarsely chopped

- 1½ tablespoons green cardamom pods

- 1²/₃ cups (13 fl oz/400 ml) sweetened condensed milk

- 3 cups (24 fl oz/750 ml) heavy (double) cream

- Rich Sauce (page 110) for serving

In a food processor, puree mango until smooth. Remove to a large bowl. In a spice grinder, grind cardamom to a powder and add to mango.

Add condensed milk and cream to mango mixture and stir until well combined; do not beat or whisk. Divide mixture among 10 ramekins with a ½-cup (4-fl oz/125-ml) capacity. Place in freezer until frozen, about 6 hours. Cover ramekins well and keep in freezer until serving.

To serve, briefly dip each ramekin in a bowl of hot water. Invert a serving plate on top and invert plate and ramekin to unmold ice cream. Top with sauce and serve immediately, decorated with thin slices of extra ripe mango, if desired.

Serves 10

Note: You can make ice cream up to 2 weeks ahead. Wrap well to prevent flavors being absorbed from other foods in freezer. Make sauce close to serving.

Carrot and cardamom milk pudding

Gajar ka halwa

Ingredients

2 lb (1 kg) carrots, (about 9 medium), peeled and grated

8 cups (64 fl oz/2 L) whole (full cream) milk

3 tablespoons green cardamom pods

6–8 saffron threads

1/2 cup (4 fl oz/125 ml) whole (full cream) milk, heated

1/2 cup (2 oz/60 g) sliced (flaked) almonds

1/2 cup (2 oz/60 g) pistachio nuts, sliced

1 cup (8 oz/250 g) sugar

1/3 cup (2 oz/60 g) raisins

2/3 cup (5 oz/150 g) ghee or unsalted butter

Preheat oven to 350°F (180°C/Gas 4).

In a large, heavy saucepan, combine carrots and 8 cups milk and bring to a boil over medium–high heat. Reduce heat to medium and cook, uncovered, stirring often, until most of milk is absorbed and carrots are soft, about 1¼ hours.

While carrots are cooking, grind cardamom to a powder in a spice grinder. Set aside.

In a bowl, combine saffron and hot milk and set aside for 10 minutes.

Spread almonds and pistachios on a baking sheet and toast in oven, stirring nuts occasionally, for 6–8 minutes. Remove from oven and let cool.

Add cardamom, saffron mixture, sugar and raisins to carrot mixture, and cook, stirring, until sugar dissolves. Simmer, uncovered, stirring often, until all liquid is absorbed, about 45 minutes.

Add ghee or butter, a spoonful at a time, stirring until combined. Cook, stirring often, until pudding begins to pull away from sides of pan, 10–15 minutes. Stir in three-fourths of nuts. Spoon into bowls and sprinkle with remaining nuts. Serve warm.

Serves 10

Note: You can spread pudding evenly in a shallow 8-inch (20-cm) square baking pan lined with plastic wrap. Refrigerate until cold. Use plastic wrap to lift pudding from pan. Cut pudding into individual portions to serve.

Ingredients

SYRUP

4 cups (2 lb/1 kg) sugar

4 cups (32 fl oz/1 L) water

1 green cardamom pod, cracked

small pinch saffron threads

DUMPLINGS

2 cups (6 oz/180 g) whole (full cream) powdered milk

1 cup (5 oz/150 g) all-purpose (plain) flour

1/4 teaspoon ground cardamom

about 1 cup (8 fl oz/250 ml) heavy (double) cream

6 cups (48 fl oz/1.5 L) vegetable oil

Step-by-step cottage cheese dumplings in syrup
Gulab jamun

To make syrup: In a large saucepan, combine sugar, water, cardamom pod and saffron. Stir over low heat until sugar dissolves. Keep warm over low heat.

1. To make dumplings: In a large bowl, combine powdered milk, flour and ground cardamom. Add cream and, using your hands, gradually incorporate flour mixture into cream to form a soft dough, adding a little more cream if dough is a bit dry. Knead lightly in bowl until smooth.

2. Shape mixture into 20 walnut-sized balls, making sure surface of each ball is very smooth. If necessary, brush balls very lightly with water and smooth over any cracks.

In a large saucepan, heat oil over medium heat to 350°F (180°C) on a deep-frying thermometer. Fry dumplings in four batches in hot oil, gently stirring them occasionally with a large slotted spoon (do not marr surface), until uniformly golden brown, 3–5 minutes. Remove to paper towels to drain for 2 minutes, then add to warm syrup. Soak in syrup for at least 30 minutes. Serve warm.

Serves 10

Note: Always serve two or more dumplings per person as it is considered rude to offer only one.

1
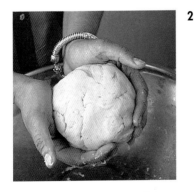

2

Ingredients

pinch saffron threads

²/₃ cup (5 fl oz/150 ml) milk, heated

3 tablespoons green cardamom pods

8 cups (4 lb/2 kg) plain (natural) whole-milk yogurt

½ cup (3½ oz/105 g) superfine (caster) sugar

crushed ice for serving

Chilled yogurt drink

Lassi

In a bowl, combine saffron and warm milk and set aside for 10 minutes. In a spice grinder, grind cardamom to a powder.

In a large bowl, combine saffron mixture, cardamom, yogurt and sugar. Whisk thoroughly until sugar dissolves and mixture begins to froth.

Pour into glasses, add crushed ice and serve immediately.

Serves 10

Note: You can thin lassi by adding milk.

Green mango drink

Panha

Ingredients

2 lb (1 kg) unripe green mangoes

3 tablespoons green cardamom pods

½ cup (4 oz/125 g) sugar

pinch salt

8 cups (64 fl oz/2 L) ice-cold water

crushed ice for serving

Rinse mangoes and place in a large saucepan. Add enough water to cover and bring to a simmer over medium heat. Cook, partially covered, until mangoes are soft and mushy, 20–30 minutes. Drain and reserve cooking water. Set mangoes aside to cool.

In a spice grinder, grind cardamom to a powder. Set aside.

Remove mango pulp from skins and pits. Place pulp in a blender with cardamom, sugar and salt. Puree until smooth, adding some cooking water if necessary to facilitate blending.

Remove mango puree to a bowl and combine with ice-cold water. Taste and adjust sugar and salt if necessary. Pour into tall glasses and add crushed ice. Serve immediately.

Serves 10

Note: As a variation, omit cardamom and add 1 teaspoon ground, dry-roasted cumin seeds and a handful of fresh mint leaves.

Ingredients

1½ tablespoons green cardamom
  pods

8 cups (64 fl oz/2 L) ice-cold water

juice of 6 lemons

⅓ cup (2 oz/60 g) superfine (caster)
  sugar or to taste

1 teaspoon black salt

pinch table salt

crushed ice for serving

Sweet lemon drink

Nimbu pani

In a spice grinder, grind cardamom to a powder. In a bowl, combine cardamom with ice-cold water, lemon juice, sugar, black salt and table salt, and whisk well until sugar dissolves.

Pour into tall glasses and add crushed ice. Serve immediately.

Serves 10

Note: As a variation, use 10 limes in place of lemons. Omit black salt if it is unavailable as there is no substitute.

Meera's masala chai (Meera's Indian tea)

Ingredients

4 cups (32 fl oz/1 L) cold water

4 teaspoons finely grated fresh ginger

⅓ cup (1 oz/30 g) tea leaves

3 tablespoons milk, plus milk for serving

½ teaspoon Garam Masala (page 28)

sugar to taste

In a saucepan, combine water and ginger and bring to a boil over medium heat. Reduce heat and stir in tea leaves. Bring to a boil again and stir in 3 tablespoons milk and garam masala.

Remove from heat and cover pan. Set aside for 4 minutes. Strain and add sugar to taste. Serve with extra milk.

Serves 8

Note: Indians generally drink their chai strong with lots of milk and sugar, but you can vary the amounts depending on how strong or diluted you like your chai. As a variation, use ground cardamom instead of garam masala.

Glossary

Almonds Almonds are mainly grown in Kashmir, in the north of India. The almond tree can grow to around 50 feet (15 m) and the almond kernel is the seed of the fruit. This oval shaped, brown-skinned nut ranges in size from 1–1½ inches (2–4 cm) and has a delicate and slightly sweet flavor. Almonds are used mostly in Moghul recipes such as biryani, ice cream, korma (where ground almonds act as a thickener) and barfi (a fudge-like sweet). They are most often blanched to remove the skins then used either whole, sliced or ground—toasted or untoasted, depending on the dish.

Buttermilk Milk that has been cultured to give it a slightly acidic, tangy flavor and a thick texture. Marinating chicken in buttermilk, such as in the Chicken Chettinad recipe, helps to tenderize it due to the action of the acids in the milk. Buttermilk is low in fat.

Cucumber The preferred cucumber to use in Indian dishes is the small, tender-skinned green cucumber variously called Lebanese, European, Greek or Cypriot. It is sometimes available in Middle Eastern markets, specialty produce markets and farmers' markets. The English (hothouse) cucumber is the best substitute. If using standard green cucumbers, commonly called salad cucumbers, select the youngest and firmest specimens possible; if using a mature cucumber, peel, halve lengthwise and scoop out the seeds.

Dates The fresh fruit of the date palm has brown skin which looks a little wrinkly and its soft flesh is golden to light brown with a deliciously sweet flavor. We used the dried variety in the Date Chutney in this book. However, in India, fresh dates are also very popular. In the muslim community, dates are often snacked upon to break the fast each day during Ramadan.

Deghchi Also known as dekchi, this is a thick-based saucepan which is quite large but shallower than the usual large saucepan and traditionally has rounded sides. It's perfect for making many of the saucy dishes in this book—make sure it has a tight-fitting lid to prevent excess evaporation of liquid. Use a regular large, shallow thick-based saucepan with a tight-fitting lid if not available.

Ghee A term that refers to pure butterfat, also called clarified butter. Most recipes in this book call for a mixture of vegetable oil and melted unsalted butter instead of ghee, as this mixture has a less imposing flavor than ghee, which is very rich. When a recipe calls for ghee, you can purchase it in tubs from Indian markets and in specialty food stores. To make your own clarified butter, place pieces of unsalted butter in a small saucepan over low heat. After the butter melts, bring to a simmer and cook for 10 minutes to evaporate any water in the butter. Skim off any froth from the top of butter and then simmer for a further 5–10 minutes or until milk solids turn light brown. Set aside to settle for 30 minutes then pour off the liquid butter into a container, discarding the browned milk solids left. Clarified butter can be stored for up to 3 months in an airtight container in the refrigerator. Ghee is used in many Indian sweets such as the Gajar Ka Halwa in this book, and is used often for general cooking in savory dishes. It gives quite a rich flavor to dishes, both sweet and savory.

Karhai Also known as kadai or kadhai, this heavy metal pan is shaped like a bowl, with handles on either side. It resembles a wok, which may be used in its place for general cooking and deep-frying. Karhai are available in Indian markets and some kitchenware stores.

Pistachio nuts Being the most expensive nut in India, pistachios are used in special occasion dishes. The use of this imported nut began during the Moghul reign and they feature often in sweets and desserts such as the Saffron and Pista Kulfi in this book. Pistachios have a vivid green color and mild creamy flavor and are used whole, chopped or ground.

Split yellow peas Called matar dal in India, these peas are used in dal recipes and as the basis for vegetarian soups. They are simply dried regular peas and are readily available from health food stores and some supermarkets. Split peas have a mild flavor and when well cooked, a mushy texture. If the yellow split peas are not

available, you can use split green peas instead, although the color and flavor will differ a little.

Tawa A flat iron hotplate, either square or round, used for cooking roti and dosai. See Masala Dosai for instructions on seasoning the tawa. You can use a heavy flat griddle instead.

Index

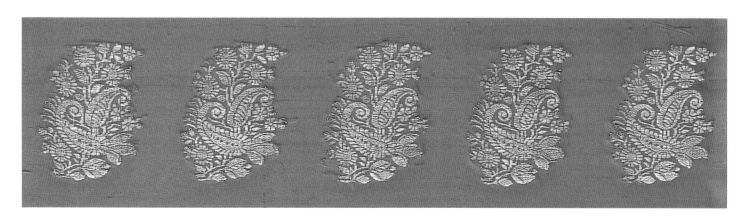

Guide to weights and measures

The conversions given in the recipes in this book are approximate. Whichever system you use, remember to follow it consistently, thereby ensuring that the proportions are consistent throughout a recipe.

WEIGHTS

Imperial	Metric
⅓ oz	10 g
½ oz	15 g
¾ oz	20 g
1 oz	30 g
2 oz	60 g
3 oz	90 g
4 oz (¼ lb)	125 g
5 oz (⅓ lb)	150 g
6 oz	180 g
7 oz	220 g
8 oz (½ lb)	250 g
9 oz	280 g
10 oz	300 g
11 oz	330 g
12 oz (¾ lb)	375 g
16 oz (1 lb)	500 g
2 lb	1 kg
3 lb	1.5 kg
4 lb	2 kg

VOLUME

Imperial	Metric	Cup
1 fl oz	30 ml	
2 fl oz	60 ml	¼
3 fl oz	90 ml	⅓
4 fl oz	125 ml	½
5 fl oz	150 ml	⅔
6 fl oz	180 ml	¾
8 fl oz	250 ml	1
10 fl oz	300 ml	1¼
12 fl oz	375 ml	1½
13 fl oz	400 ml	1⅔
14 fl oz	440 ml	1¾
16 fl oz	500 ml	2
24 fl oz	750 ml	3
32 fl oz	1 L	4

USEFUL CONVERSIONS

¼ teaspoon	1.25 ml
½ teaspoon	2.5 ml
1 teaspoon	5 ml
1 Australian tablespoon	20 ml (4 teaspoons)
1 UK/US tablespoon	15 ml (3 teaspoons)

OVEN TEMPERATURE GUIDE

The Celsius (°C) and Fahrenheit (°F) temperatures in this chart apply to most electric ovens. Decrease by 25°F (10°C) for a gas oven or refer to the manufacturer's temperature guide. For temperatures below 325°F (160°C), do not decrease the given temperature.

Oven description	°C	°F	Gas Mark
Cool	110	225	¼
	130	250	½
Very slow	140	275	1
	150	300	2
Slow	170	325	3
Moderate	180	350	4
	190	375	5
Moderately Hot	200	400	6
Fairly Hot	220	425	7
Hot	230	450	8
Very Hot	240	475	9
Extremely Hot	250	500	10

Osso Bosso

2 tbsp olive oil

4 Veal Shanks (sear/brown)

1 C (onion, carrots, celery) (Sautee)

1 tsp (pinch) salt & pepper

2 cups white wine

3 cups beef or chicken broth

juice of one lemon } at
zest of one lemon } end of
cooking

bake covered at 350° for